THE
OFFICIAL
theory
test for motorcyclists

VALID FOR TESTS TAKEN FROM 4TH SEPTEMBER 2000

London: The Stationery Office

Written and compiled by the Publications Unit of the Driving Standards Agency (DSA)

Questions and answers are compiled by the Question Development Team of the DSA with support from the National Foundation for Educational Research

Published by The Stationery Office with the permission of the Controller of Her Majesty's Stationery Office on behalf of the Driving Standards Agency.

First published 2000

ISBN 0 11 552223 9

A CIP catalogue record for this book is available from the British Library

Other titles in the Driving series

The Official Theory Test for Car Drivers and Motorcyclists
The Official Theory Test for Drivers of Large Vehicles
The Official Motorcycling Manual
The Official Driving Manual
The Official Guide to Compulsory Basic Training for Motorcyclists
The Official DSA Guide for Driving Instructors
The Official Bus and Coach Driving Manual
The Official Goods Vehicle Driving Manual
The Official Guide to Tractor and Specialist Vehicle Driving Tests
The Official Driving Test
The Official Theory Test CD-ROM – 'Your Licence to Drive'
The Official Guide to Accompanying Learner Drivers

DSA THEORY TEST for motorcyclists

ACKNOWLEDGEMENTS

The Driving Standards Agency would like to thank their staff and the following organisations for their contribution to the production of this publication.

National Foundation for Educational Research

Transport Research Laboratory

Department of Environment, Transport and the Regions

Driver & Vehicle Testing Agency, Northern Ireland

Every effort has been made to ensure that the information contained in this publication is accurate at the time of going to press. The Stationery Office cannot be held responsible for any inaccuracies.

Information in this book is for guidance only.

All metric and imperial conversions in this book are approximate.

Information

Theory Test
DSA Bookings and Enquiries: 0870 01 01 372
DVTA (Northern Ireland) Booking and Enquiries: 0845 6006700

Faxes: 0870 01 04 372
Minicom: 0870 01 06 372
Welsh speakers: 0870 01 00 372

Postal applications to:
Driving Standards Agency or Driver and Vehicle Testing Agency
PO Box 148
Salford M5 3SY

Driving Standards Agency:
(Headquarters)
Stanley House
Talbot Street
Nottingham NG1 5GU

Tel: 0115 901 2500
Fax: 0115 901 2510

Driver & Vehicle Testing Agency
(Headquarters)
Balmoral Road
Belfast BT12 6QL

Tel: 02890 681831
Fax: 02890 665520

Driver Vehicle Licensing Authority
(GB Licence Enquiries)

Tel: 01792 772151
Fax: 01792 783071
Minicom: 01792 782787

Driver and Vehicle Licensing Northern Ireland
Customer Services
Tel: 02870 341469
02890 250 500 (24 hours)
Minicom: 02870 341 380

Website addresses:
DSA: www.driving-tests.co.uk
DVTA: www.doeni.gov.uk/dvta

DSA THEORY TEST for motorcyclists

The Driving Standards Agency (DSA) is an executive agency of the Department of the Environment, Transport and the Regions (DETR).

You'll see its logo at test centres.

DSA aims to promote road safety through the advancement of driving standards, by

- establishing and developing high standards and best practice in driving and riding on the road; before people start to drive, as they learn, and after they pass their test
- ensuring high standards of instruction for different types of driver and rider
- conducting the statutory theory and practical tests efficiently, fairly and consistently across the country
- providing a centre of excellence for driver training and driving standards
- developing a range of publications and other publicity material designed to promote safe driving for life.

DVTA

The Driver & Vehicle Testing Agency (DVTA) is an executive agency within the Department of the Environment for Northern Ireland. Its primary aim is to promote and improve road safety

through the advancement of driving standards and implementation of the Government's policies for improving the mechanical standards of vehicles.

DSA Website

www.driving-tests.co.uk

DVTA Website

www.doeni.gov.uk/dvta

"... but what about the insurance ?"

No problem, just call Carole Nash

0800 298 5500

CAROLE NASH
INSURANCE CONSULTANTS LTD

Open 8-6.30 Mon-Fri 9-12 Sat Instant cover & free breakdown recovery on all policies.
www.carolenash.com. email: bikes@carolenash.com
IRISH POLICIES AVAILABLE N. Ireland: 0800 298 5500 Ireland: Dublin 636 9191

CONTENTS

DSA **THEORY TEST** for motorcyclists

With the ever-increasing volume of traffic on the roads today, it's important to make sure that new riders have a broad spread of riding knowledge. New motorcycle riders are required to pass a separate theory test before obtaining a full motorcycle licence. This is a major step towards improving road safety in the UK.

This book is intended to help new riders prepare for the theory test. An extensive knowledge of riding theory will help towards a better understanding of practical riding skills. This is necessary to become a safe and confident rider.

This book contains the motorcycle theory test question bank, set out in an easy-to-read style with plenty of illustrations. To assist preparation for the test it explains why the answers are correct and identifies good riding practice.

These other books in the Driving Skills series will help you to develop your motorcycling skills:

The Highway Code

Know Your Traffic Signs

The Official Driving Manuual

The Official Motorcycling Manual

The Official Guide to Compulsory Basic Training and the Motorcycle Test.

Both are published by The Stationery Office.

Robin Cummins
The Chief Driving Examiner
Driving Standards Agency

This book tells you about the touch screen theory test. It will help you to

- study for your theory test
- prepare and be successful.

Part One gives you information on how to get started.

Part Two tells you about the test itself.

Part Three shows you the questions that may be used in your test. Don't worry, you won't have to answer all of them. Your test will have 35 questions.

Books for study

To prepare properly for the theory test DSA strongly recommends that you study the books from which the questions are taken. These books, known as the source material, these consist of: *The Highway Code, Know Your Traffic Signs, The Official Guide to Compulsory Basic Training* and *The Official Motorcycling Manual.*

These books will help you to answer the questions correctly and will also guide you when studying for your practical test. Keep them so that you can refer to them regulary. You can find them in most booksellers, together with relevant books from other publishers. Information about these, and other DSA products, appears at the back of this book.

The Driving Standards Agency has also produced a CD ROM containing all the questions, which allows you to practise mock theory tests.

It's important that you study – not just to pass the test but to become a safe rider.

To ensure that all candidates are tested fairly, questions used in the theory test are under continuous review. *Some of the questions used will be changed periodically to reflect changes in legislation, or as a result of customer feedback. There may be questions in your test that do not appear in this book.* The information needed to answer all questions is readily available in the books recommended for study on the previous page.

Riding is a life skill.

Your tests are just the beginning.

When you pass your theory test you will be given a certificate. **This is valid for two years from the date of your test.** You will have to take and pass your practical test within this two-year period. If you don't, you will have to take and pass the theory test again before a booking for a practical test can be accepted.

Some of the questions in this book will not be used in Northern Ireland theory tests.

 These questions are marked with this symbol.

Compulsory Basic Training

Before you take your practical motorcycle test you must attend and successfully complete a Compulsory Basic Training (CBT) course (except in Northern Ireland). CBT courses can only be given by training bodies approved by DSA. Frequent checks are made to ensure a high standard of instruction.

The course will include
• classroom training
• practical skills training.

You can find out about CBT courses from
• DSA Tel: **0115 901 2595**
• your motorcycle dealer
• your local Road Safety Officer (by contacting your local council)

DSA also produces *The Official Guide to Compulsory Basic Training for Motorcyclists*, which will give you details about the course.

You'll have to answer specific questions on motorcycling in the theory test. DSA's *The Official Motorcycling Manual* tells you about motorcycling skills in more detail. Books from other publishers are also available. In addition, you should buy and study a copy of *The Highway Code, The Driving Manual,* and *Know Your Traffic Signs.*

Keep them and refer to them after you've passed your tests. Make sure that you have the latest copy of *The Highway Code* as it's updated periodically.

Information about these and other DSA products appears at the back of this book.

Applying for your licence

You'll need to apply for a provisional driving licence, as you must produce it at the theory test centre. An application form D1 (DL1 in Northern Ireland) can be obtained from any post office.

When you receive your photocard provisional licence, check that all the details are correct. Don't drive until you've done so.

Residency requirements

You can't take a test or obtain a full licence unless you are normally resident in this country. Normal residence means the place where you reside because of personal or occupational ties. If you moved to the United Kingdom (UK) having recently been permanently resident in another state of the EC/EEA (European Economic Area), you must have been normally resident in the UK for 185 days in the 12 months prior to your application for a driving test or full driving licence.

About the theory test

During your test questions will appear on a computer screen. You will select your answers by simply touching the screen.

This 'touch screen' system has been carefully designed to make it easy to use.

You can work through a practice session to get used to the system before starting your test. Staff at the test centre will be on hand to help you if you have any difficulties.

The screens are easy to read. Only one question will appear on the screen at a time. You will be able to move backwards and forwards through the questions. You will also be able to 'flag' questions that you want to look at again. It is easy to change your answer.

Some questions ask you to select more than one answer option. The system will alert you if you have not completely answered a question.

Does everyone have to take the theory test?

Foreign licence holders:

If you hold a foreign driving licence issued outside the EEA, first check with the Driver and Vehicle Licencing Agency (Tel: **01792 772151**) whether you can exchange your driving licence. If you cannot exchange your licence, you will need to take a theory and practical driving test.

Any particular enquiries about whether a theory test is required should be addressed to the

Theory Test Unit,
Driving Standards Agency,
Stanley House,
56 Talbot Street,
Nottingham, NG1 5GU
Tel: 0115 901 2500.

Can I take my practical test first?

No. You have to take and pass your theory test before a booking for the practical test is accepted.

How many questions are there?

There are 35 questions in the test. You should try to answer all of them. To pass you must answer at least 30 questions correctly.

How long do I have to complete the test?

Each test session lasts for 40 minutes. You can take all this time if you need to. The time remaining for your test is displayed on screen.

Where do I have to go to take the test?

There are over 150 test centres throughout England, Scotland, Wales and Northern Ireland. Most people have a test centre within 20 miles of their home, but this will vary depending on the density of the population in your area. You can find a list of test centres at the back of this book.

When are the test centres open?

Sessions are provided on weekdays, evenings and on Saturdays. However, where demand is less than 100 tests per year test sessions may be less frequent.

Will I know the result straight away?

Not straight away but you should receive your result at the test centre within 30 minutes of completing the test.

If I don't pass, when can I take the theory test again?

You will have to wait a minimum of three clear working days before you take the theory test again. If you fail your test you've shown that you aren't fully prepared. Good preparation will save you time and money.

Is the test only available in English?

No. The test is available in English and the following languages

Albanian	Gujarati	Spanish
Arabic	Hindi	Tamil
Bengali	Kurdish	Turkish
Cantonese	Portuguese	Urdu
Farsi	Punjabi	Welsh

You will be able to listen through a headset to the test being read out in any of these languages.

Northern Ireland tests are available in Cantonese, Bengali and Urdu only.

Can I bring a translator with me?

Yes. If you don't speak any of the languages available you're allowed to bring a DSA or DVTA approved translator with you when you take your test. The Special Needs team at the booking office will tell you who is approved. When you have made arrangements with the translator you should tell the booking office who you intend to bring with you.

If you bring an approved translator with you the responsibility for the contractual arrangements, including the fee charged, is between you and the translator.

Are there any provisions for special needs?

Every effort has been made to ensure that the theory test can be taken by all candidates. It's important that you state your needs when booking so that the necessary arrangements can be made.

There is an English language voiceover, on a headset, to support candidates with dyslexia and other reading difficulties. You can also ask for up to double the normal time to take the test. As evidence of this requirement you will be asked to provide a letter from a teacher or educationalist, a psychologist or a doctor (if appropriate). If it isn't possible to get this confirmation from a relevant professional, DSA, or DVTA, will consider a letter from an independent person who knows about your reading ability. This could be your employer, but if you are unsure about who to ask please telephone the Special Needs section on **0870 01 01 372** (Fax **0820 01 04 372**) or on **0845 600 6700** in Northern Ireland.

DSA and DVTA are unable to take responsibility for the safe return of any original documentation sent, so it is advisable to send copies only.

A test with video in British Sign Language is available on screen for candidates who are deaf or who have other hearing difficulties. A BSL interpreter or lip speaker can be provided if requested at the time of booking.

If you require wheelchair access and your nearest test centre doesn't provide this, DSA or DVTA will arrange for you to take the test at a location suitable for you, such as a library or job centre, or take you to another test centre where the facilities are provided.

How do I book a test?

The easiest way to book a test is by telephone, using your credit or debit card. The person who books the test must be the card-holder.

If you book by this method you'll be given the date and time of your test immediately. You can do this by calling **0870 01 01 372** or **0845 600 6700** for Northern Ireland at any time between 8 am and 6 pm Monday to Friday. When you phone you should have ready your

* DVLA/DVLNI driving licence number
* credit or debit card details.

If you're deaf and need a minicom machine telephone **0870 01 06 372**.

Welsh speakers can telephone **0870 01 00 372**.

You'll be given a booking number, and sent an appointment letter that you should expect to receive within four days of your call. If not please contact the booking office to check that the appointment was made.

Alternatively you can book a test by post. Application forms are available from

* theory test centres
* driving test centres
* your Approved Training Body.

You should receive an appointment letter within 10 days of posting your application form. If not, please telephone the booking office to check that your application was received and that a test appointment has been made.

DSA and DVTA cannot take responsibility for postal delays, If you miss your test appointment you will lose your fee.

How do I cancel or postpone a test?

To cancel or postpone a theory test appointment you should contact the booking office at least **three clear working days** before the test date, otherwise you will lose your fee. Only in exceptional circumstances like documented ill-health or family bereavement can this rule be waived.

At the test centre

Make sure that you have all the necessary documents with you. You'll need

- both parts of your signed photocard licence, or
- your signed driving licence and photo identity.

The form of photographic identification acceptable at both theory and practical tests is as follows

- **your photocard driving licence**
- **your passport**, which doesn't have to be a British passport
- *****cheque guarantee card or credit card** bearing your photograph and signature
- **an employer's identity or workplace pass** bearing your photograph and name or signature or both
- **Trade Union Card** bearing your photograph and signature
- **Student Union Card** with reference to either the NUS or an education establishment/course reference number. The card must bear your photograph and name or signature or both
- **School Bus Pass** bearing the name of the issuing authority and your photograph and signature

- *****card issued in connection with sale and purchase of reduced-price railway tickets** bearing the name of the issuing authority and your photograph and signature. This is a card issued by a Railway Authority or other authorised body to purchase a reduced-price railway ticket (e.g. a Young Persons Railcard)
- *****Gun Licence**, including a Firearm or Shotgun Certificate, which bears your photograph and signature
- *****Proof of Age Card** issued by the Portman Group bearing your photograph and signature

Remember...

No photo
   No licence
      No test

*Not valid in Northern Ireland.

If you don't have any of these you can bring a signed photograph, together with a statement like the one shown below, that it's a true likeness of you. Both the statement, and the back of the photograph must be signed by the same person. This can be any of the following

- *Approved Driving Instructor, but not a trainee (pink licence) holder
- *DSA-certified motorcycle instructor
- Member of Parliament
- medical practitioner
- *local authority councillor
- teacher (qualified)
- Justice of the Peace
- civil servant (established)
- police officer
- bank official
- minister of religion
- barrister or solicitor
- *Commissioned Officer in Her Majesty's Forces
- *LGV Trainers on the DSA Voluntary Register of LGV Instructors.

*Not valid in Northern Ireland.

If you don't bring these documents on the day, you won't be able to take your test and you'll lose your fee. If you have any queries about what photographic evidence we will accept, contact the enquiry line on **0870 01 01 372** or **0845 600 6700** in Northern Ireland.

Arrive in plenty of time so that you aren't rushed. The test centre staff will check your documents and ensure that you receive the right category test. If you arrive after the session has started you may not be allowed to sit the test.

I (name of certifier), certify that this is a true likeness of , who has been known to me for (number) months / years in my capacity as

Signed
Dated
Daytime phone no.
ADI/CBT Instructor no.

The Touch Screen Test

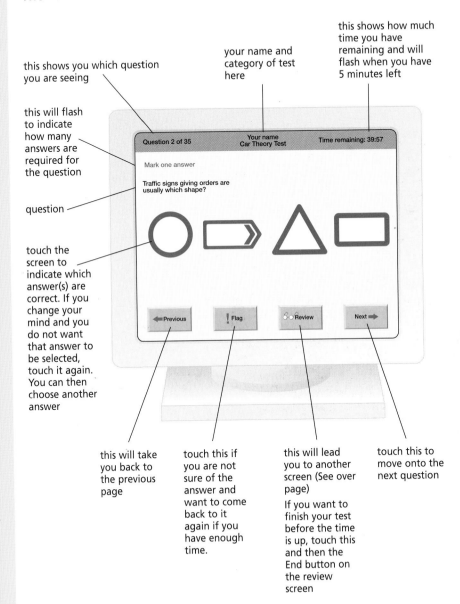

this shows how much time you have remaining and will flash when you have 5 minutes left

your name and category of test here

this shows you which question you are seeing

this will flash to indicate how many answers are required for the question

question

touch the screen to indicate which answer(s) are correct. If you change your mind and you do not want that answer to be selected, touch it again. You can then choose another answer

Question 2 of 35

Your name
Car Theory Test

Time remaining: 39:57

Mark one answer

Traffic signs giving orders are usually which shape?

Previous | Flag | Review | Next

this will take you back to the previous page

touch this if you are not sure of the answer and want to come back to it again if you have enough time.

this will lead you to another screen (See over page)

If you want to finish your test before the time is up, touch this and then the End button on the review screen

touch this to move onto the next question

Reviewing questions

When you press the review button you will see this screen.

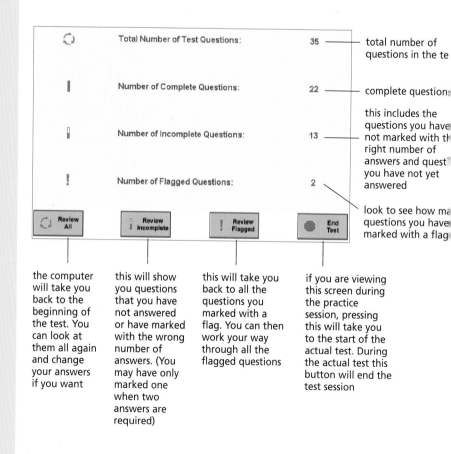

total number of questions in the te

complete question

this includes the questions you have not marked with th right number of answers and quest you have not yet answered

look to see how m questions you have marked with a flag

the computer will take you back to the beginning of the test. You can look at them all again and change your answers if you want

this will show you questions that you have not answered or have marked with the wrong number of answers. (You may have only marked one when two answers are required)

this will take you back to all the questions you marked with a flag. You can then work your way through all the flagged questions

if you are viewing this screen during the practice session, pressing this will take you to the start of the actual test. During the actual test this button will end the test session

When you have finished your test you may be shown some trial questions. These help us to see if we will use them in future theory tests. They **do not** count towards your final score.

We want to ensure that customers are completely satisfied with the level of service we provide. You will be shown some questions designed to give us some information about you and how satisfied you are with the service you have received from us. Your answers will be treated in strictest confidence. They are **not** part of the test and will not be used in determining your final score. You will be given a choice of whether you wish to complete the survey.

Test Content

At the start of the test you'll have the opportunity to complete some practise questions.

Most questions will ask you to mark ONE correct answer from four. Other questions will ask for TWO OR MORE correct answers from a selection. Some of the questions will show you a picture. This is to test your knowledge of traffic signs or your ability to spot a hazard. Look at the question carefully.

The questions will cover a variety of topics relating to road safety. Touch the box alongside the answers you think are correct.

Some questions will take longer to answer than others. There are no trick questions. If you're well prepared you won't find them difficult.

Take your time and read the questions carefully. You're given plenty of time, so relax and don't rush. Try to answer all 35 questions.

When you think you've finished, use the 'review' feature to check your answers before you end your test.

About Part Three

In this part of the book you'll find questions that might be used in your theory test. The answers have been provided to help you to study.

For easy reference and to help you to study, the questions have been divided into topics and put into sections. Although this isn't how you'll find them in your test it's helpful if you want to refer to particular subjects.

The questions are in the left-hand column with a choice of answers beneath. On the right-hand side of the page you'll find the correct answers and a brief explanation of why they are correct. There will also be some advice on correct driving procedures.

DON'T JUST LEARN THE ANSWERS. It's important that you know **why** the answers are correct. This will help you with your practical skills and prepare you to become a safe and confident rider

Taking exams or tests is rarely a pleasant experience, but you can make your test less stressful by being confident that you have the knowledge to answer the questions correctly.

Make studying more fun by involving friends and relations. Take part in a question-and-answer game. Test those 'experienced' riders and drivers who've had their licence a while: they might learn something too!

SECTION 1 ALERTNESS

This section looks at alertness and attention
when you're riding.

The questions will ask you about

- **Observation**

  look all around for other road users and pedestrians.

- **Anticipation**

  look ahead and giving yourself enough time to react
  to hazards.

- **Concentration**

  be alert at all times when riding.

- **Awareness**

  understand the actions of other road users.

- **Distraction**

  don't become distracted whilst riding. Your
  attention must be on the road.

- **Boredom**

  could make you feel sleepy. Keep your
  mind on your riding.

Question 1.1

Mark one answer

Before you make a U-turn in the road, you should

- give an arm signal as well as using your indicators
- signal so that other drivers can slow down for you
- look over your shoulder for a final check
- select a higher gear than normal

Answer

- **look over your shoulder for a final check**

If you want to make a U-turn, slow down and ensure that the road is clear in both directions. Make sure that the road is wide enough to carry out the manoeuvre safely.

Question 1.2

Mark one answer

To move off safely from a parked position you should

- signal if other drivers will need to slow down
- leave your motorcycle on its stand until the road is clear
- give an arm signal as well as using your indicators
- look over your shoulder for a final check

Answer

- **look over your shoulder for a final check**

If you're intending to move off from the side of the road on a motorcycle you must take a final look around over your shoulder. There may be another road user not visible in your mirrors.

Question 1.3

Mark one answer

When riding, your shoulders obstruct the view in your mirrors. To overcome this you should

- indicate earlier than normal
- fit smaller mirrors
- extend the mirror arms
- brake earlier than normal

Answer

- **extend the mirror arms**

It's essential that you have a clear view all around. Check the position of the mirrors before you move off.

Question 1.4

Mark two answers

You want to change lanes in busy, moving traffic. Why could looking over your shoulder help?

- Mirrors may not cover blind spots
- To avoid having to give a signal
- So traffic ahead will make room for you
- So your balance will not be affected
- Following motorists would be warned

Answers

- **Mirrors may not cover blind spots**
- **Following motorists would be warned**

Before you change lanes you need to know that there's a safe gap to move into. Looking over your shoulder

- allows you to see into the area not covered by the mirrors and which could hide another vehicle
- warns following motorists that you want to change lanes.

Question 1.5

Mark one answer

You are about to turn right. What should you do just before you turn?

- Give the correct signal
- Take a 'lifesaver' glance over your shoulder
- Select the correct gear
- Get in position ready for the turn

Answer

- **Take a 'lifesaver' glance over your shoulder**

When you're turning right, plan your approach to the junction. Signal and select the correct gear in good time. Just before you turn give a 'lifesaver' glance to the rear for a final check behind and alongside.

Question 1.6

Mark one answer

What is the 'lifesaver' when riding a motorcycle?

- A certificate every motorcyclist must have
- A final, rearward glance before changing direction
- A part of the motorcycle tool kit
- A mirror fitted to check blind spots

Answer

- **A final, rearward glance before changing direction**

This action makes you aware of what's happening behind and alongside. This glance should be timed so that you still have time to react if it isn't safe to perform the manoeuvre.

DSA THEORY TEST for motorcyclists

Question 1.7

Mark one answer

You see road signs showing a sharp bend ahead. What should you do?

- [ ] Continue at the same speed
- [ ] Slow down as you go around the bend
- [ ] Slow down as you come out of the bend
- [ ] Slow down before the bend

Answer

- [ ] **Slow down before the bend**

Road signs might give you warning of a hazard ahead. Always look and plan well ahead. This will avoid the need for late, harsh braking. Your motorcycle should be upright and moving in a straight line when you brake. This will ensure maximum control when dealing with the hazard.

Question 1.8

Mark three answers

As you approach this bridge you should

- [ ] move into the middle of the road to get a better view
- [ ] slow down
- [ ] get over the bridge as quickly as possible
- [ ] consider using your horn
- [ ] find another route
- [ ] beware of pedestrians

Answer

- [ ] **slow down**
- [ ] **consider using your horn**
- [ ] **beware of pedestrians**

This sign gives you a warning. You can't see over the bridge for oncoming traffic, so you must be cautious; slow right down. Consider the hidden hazards and be ready to react if necessary.

Mark one answer

When following a large vehicle you should keep well back because

- ▪ it allows you to corner more quickly
- ▪ it helps the large vehicle to stop more easily
- ▪ it allows the driver to see you in the mirrors
- ▪ it helps you to keep out of the wind

Answer

▪ **it allows the driver to see you in the mirrors**

You also need to keep well back so that you get the best view of the road ahead.

Question 1.10

Mark one answer

In which of these situations should you avoid overtaking?

- ▪ Just after a bend
- ▪ In a one-way street
- ▪ On a 30 mph road
- ▪ Approaching a dip in the road

Answer

▪ **Approaching a dip in the road**

As you begin to think about overtaking ask yourself if it's really necessary. If you can't see well down the road stay back and wait for a safer place to pull out.

Question 1.11

Mark one answer

This road marking warns

- ▪ drivers to use the hard shoulder
- ▪ overtaking drivers there is a bend to the left
- ▪ overtaking drivers to move back to the left
- ▪ drivers that it is safe to overtake

Answer

▪ **overtaking drivers to move back to the left**

You should plan your overtaking to take into consideration any hazards ahead. In this picture the marking indicates that you are approaching a junction. You will not have time to overtake and move back into the left safely.

Question 1.12

Mark one answer

Your mobile phone rings while you are travelling. You should

- stop immediately
- answer it immediately
- pull up in a suitable place
- pull up at the nearest kerb

Answer

pull up in a suitable place

Always use the safe option. It is not worth taking the risk of endangering other road users. Make sure that you pull up in a place that does not obstruct other road users. The use of a message service can enable you to complete your journey without interruptions and you can catch up with your calls when you take your rest breaks.

Question 1.13

Mark one answer

You are riding at night. You have your headlight on main beam. Another vehicle is overtaking you. When should you dip your headlight?

- When the other vehicle signals to overtake
- As soon as the other vehicle moves out to overtake
- As soon as the other vehicle passes you
- After the other vehicle pulls in front of you

Answer

As soon as the other vehicle passes you

At night you should dip your headlamp to avoid dazzling

- oncoming drivers
- drivers in front.

If you're being overtaken, dip your headlamp as the other vehicle comes past. When you dip you'll see less of the road, so look ahead for hazards on your side of the road before dipping.

Question 1.14

Mark one answer

On a motorcycle you should only use a mobile telephone when you

- have a pillion passenger to help
- have parked in a safe place
- have a motorcycle with automatic gears
- are travelling on a quiet road

Answer

have parked in a safe place

It's important that you're in full control of your machine at all times. If you need to use a hand-held phone you must stop at a safe place before you do so.

Mark one answer

You are riding at night and are dazzled by the headlights of an oncoming car. You should

▓ slow down or stop

▓ close your eyes

▓ flash your headlight

▓ turn your head away

Answer

▓ **slow down or stop**

If you're riding a motorcycle, taking a hand off the handlebars to adjust your visor might lead to loss of control. A dirty or scratched visor could cause dazzle and impair vision further.

Whether riding slow down or stop until your eyes have adjusted.

Mark one answer

Why are these yellow lines painted across the road?

▓ To help you choose the correct lane

▓ To help you keep the correct separation distance

▓ To make you aware of your speed

▓ To tell you the distance to the roundabout

Answer

▓ **To make you aware of your speed**

These lines are often found on an approach to a roundabout or a dangerous junction. They give you extra warning to adjust your speed. Look well ahead and do this in good time.

Question 1.17

Mark one answer

You are riding along a motorway. You see
an accident on the other side of the road.
Your lane is clear. You should

- assist the emergency services
- stop, and cross the road to help
- concentrate on what is happening
  ahead
- place a warning triangle in the road

Answer

**concentrate on what is happening
ahead**

Always concentrate on the road ahead. If you
become distracted you may not see a hazard
ahead until it's too late to avoid it.

Question 1.18

Mark one answer

Which of the following should you do
before stopping your motorcycle?

- Sound the horn
- Use the mirrors
- Select a higher gear
- Flash your headlights

Answer

Use the mirrors

Before pulling up you should check for
following traffic. Also assess what is ahead
and give the correct signal if it helps another
road user.

Question 1.19

Mark one answer

You are approaching traffic lights that have
been on green for some time. You should

- accelerate hard
- maintain your speed
- be ready to stop
- brake hard

Answer

be ready to stop

The longer that traffic lights have been on
green, then the greater the chance of the
sequence changing, so always allow for
this when riding and be prepared to stop.

Mark one answer

In motorcycling, the term 'lifesaver' refers to

- a final rearward glance
- an approved safety helmet
- a reflective jacket
- the two second rule

Answer

a final rearward glance

Mirrors on motorcycles don't always give a clear view behind. There will be times when you need to look round to see the full picture

Question 1.21

Mark one answer

Riding a motorcycle when you are cold could cause you to

- be more alert
- be more relaxed
- react more quickly
- lose concentration

Answer

lose concentration

Keeping warm can be a problem. Proper motorcycle clothing isn't cheap, but it will keep you warm and is essential in cold weather. It also offers some safety benefits in the event of an accident.

Question 1.22

Mark one answer

You are riding at night and are dazzled by the lights of an approaching vehicle. What should you do?

- Switch off your headlight
- Switch to main beam
- Slow down and stop
- Flash your headlight

Answer

Slow down and stop

If your view of the road ahead is restricted because you are being dazzled by approaching headlights, then slow down and if necessary stop.

DSA THEORY TEST for motorcyclists

SECTION 2 ATTITUDE

This section looks at your attitude to other road users.

The questions will ask you about

- **Consideration**

  consider other road users. Be positive but treat them as you would wish to be treated.

- **Close following**

  don't follow too closely. As well as being dangerous, it can feel threatening to a driver in front.

- **Courtesy**

  treat other road users as colleagues or team members. They too are trying to complete their journey safely.

- **Priority**

  be aware that all rules on priority won't always be followed by other road users. Try to be calm and tolerant if other drivers or riders break the rules.

Question 2.1

Mark one answer

A pelican crossing that crosses the road in a STRAIGHT line and has a central island MUST be treated as

- one crossing in daylight only
- one complete crossing
- two separate crossings
- two crossings during darkness

Answer

- **one complete crossing**

The lights that control the crossing show to both directions of traffic. If a pedestrian from either side is still crossing when the amber light is flashing, you MUST wait.

Question 2.2

Mark one answer

You are approaching a pelican crossing. The amber light is flashing. You MUST

- give way to pedestrians who are crossing
- encourage pedestrians to cross
- not move until the green light appears
- stop even if the crossing is clear

Answer

- **give way to pedestrians who are crossing**

While the pedestrians are crossing don't

- encourage people to cross by waving or flashing your headlights – others may misunderstand your signal
- rev your engine impatiently.

Question 2.3

Mark one answer

You are riding towards a zebra crossing. Pedestrians are waiting to cross. You should

- give way to the elderly and infirm only
- slow down and prepare to stop
- use your headlight to indicate they can cross
- wave at them to cross the road

Answer

- **slow down and prepare to stop**

It's courteous to stop if you can do so safely, especially if

- anyone is waiting on the pavement with a pram or pushchair
- children or the elderly are hesitating to cross because of heavy traffic.

Mark one answer

You are approaching a red light at a puffin crossing. Pedestrians are on the crossing. The red light will stay on until

- you start to edge forward on to the crossing
- the pedestrians have reached a safe position
- the pedestrians are clear of the front of your motorcycle
- a driver from the opposite direction reaches the crossing

Answer

- **the pedestrians have reached a safe position**

The electronic device will automatically detect that the pedestrians have reached a safe position. Don't proceed until the green light shows it is safe to do so.

Question 2.5

Mark one answer

You could use the 'Two-Second Rule'

- before restarting the engine after it has stalled
- to keep a safe gap from the vehicle in front
- before using the 'Mirror–Signal–Manoeuvre' routine
- when emerging on wet roads

Answer

- **to keep a safe gap from the vehicle in front**

To measure this, choose a reference point such as a bridge, sign or tree. When the vehicle ahead passes the object say to yourself 'Only a fool breaks the Two-Second Rule.' If you reach the object before you finish saying this you're TOO CLOSE.

Question 2.6

Mark one answer

'Tailgating' means

- using the rear door of a hatchback car
- reversing into a parking space
- following another vehicle too closely
- driving with rear fog lights on

Answer

- **following another vehicle too closely**

'Tailgating' is used to describe this dangerous practice, often seen in fast-moving traffic and on motorways. Following the vehicle in front too closely will

- restrict your view of the road ahead
- leave you no safety margin if the vehicle in front stops suddenly.

Question 2.7

Mark one answer

You are following a vehicle on a wet road. You should leave a time gap of at least

- one second
- two seconds
- three seconds
- four seconds

Answer

four seconds

Wet roads will increase the time it will take you to stop. The 'Two-Second Rule' will double to AT LEAST FOUR SECONDS.

Question 2.8

Mark one answer

A long, heavily-laden lorry is taking a long time to overtake you. What should you do?

- Speed up
- Slow down
- Hold your speed
- Change direction

Answer

Slow down

A long lorry with a heavy load will need more time to pass you than a car. It won't be able to accelerate to pass you quickly, especially on an uphill stretch of road. Ease off the throttle and allow the lorry to pass.

Question 2.9

Mark one answer

You are riding a slow-moving scooter on a narrow winding road. You should

- keep well out to stop vehicles overtaking dangerously
- wave following vehicles past you if you think they can overtake quickly
- pull in safely when you can, to let following vehicles overtake
- give a left signal when it is safe for vehicles to overtake you

Answer

pull in safely when you can, to let following vehicles overtake

Don't
- wave the other traffic on – they may not have seen your signal
- show discourtesy by not pulling in at a safe place.

Try to be courteous and considerate to other road users. Imagine how you would feel if you were the following driver or rider.

Mark one answer

You are riding a slow-moving scooter on a narrow road. When traffic wishes to overtake you should

- [ ] take no action
- [ ] put your hazard warning lights on
- [ ] stop immediately and wave it on
- [ ] pull in safely as soon as you can do so

Answer

- ▊ **pull in safely as soon as you can do so**

Try not to hold up a queue of traffic. This might lead to other road users becoming impatient. If you're riding a slow-moving scooter and the road is narrow look out for a safe place to pull in.

Question 2.11

Mark one answer

You are riding a motorcycle and following a large vehicle at 40 mph. You should position yourself

- [ ] close behind to make it easier to overtake the vehicle
- [ ] to the left of the road to make it easier to be seen
- [ ] close behind the vehicle to keep out of the wind
- [ ] well back so that you can see past the vehicle

Answer

- ▊ **well back so that you can see past the vehicle**

You need to be able to see well down the road and be ready for any hazards that occur. Staying too close to the vehicle will leave you insufficient separation distance and also reduce your view of the road ahead.

Question 2.12

Mark three answers

Which THREE of these emergency services might have blue flashing beacons?

- [ ] Coastguard
- [ ] Bomb disposal
- [ ] Gritting lorries
- [ ] Animal ambulances
- [ ] Mountain rescue
- [ ] Doctors' cars

Answers

- ▊ **Coastguard**
- ▊ **Bomb disposal**
- ▊ **Mountain rescue**

These vehicles will be travelling at speed. You should help their progress by pulling over and allowing them to pass. Do so safely. Don't stop suddenly or in a dangerous position.

Question 2.13

Mark one answer

A flashing green beacon on a vehicle means

- police on non-urgent duties
- doctor on an emergency call
- road safety patrol operating
- gritting in progress

Answer

- **doctor on an emergency call**

If you see such a vehicle in your mirrors allow it to pass if you can. Be aware that someone's life could depend on the driver making good progress through traffic.

Question 2.14

Mark one answer

Diamond-shaped signs give instructions to

- tram drivers
- bus drivers
- lorry drivers
- taxi drivers

Answer

- **tram drivers**

These signs apply to trams only. They are directed at tram drivers, but you should know their meaning so that you're aware of the priorities and are able to anticipate the actions of the driver.

Question 2.15

Mark one answer

Scooter riders should be especially careful when crossing tram lines because scooters have

- small engines
- wide panniers
- automatic gear boxes
- narrow tyres

Answer

- **narrow tyres**

Tram rails can affect steering and braking, especially when wet. If you ride a small motorcycle with narrow tyres you can be affected more than riders on larger machines which have wider tyres.

Mark one answer

On a road where trams operate, which of these vehicles will be most at risk from the tram rails?

- Cars
- Cycles
- Buses
- Lorries

Answer

- Cycles

The narrow tyres of a cycle can become stuck in the tram rails. This could cause the cyclist to wobble or even lose balance altogether. The tram lines are also slippery and this could cause a cyclist to slide or fall off.

Question 2.17

Mark one answer

A bus is stopped at a bus stop ahead of you. Its right-hand indicator is flashing. You should

- flash your headlights and slow down
- slow down and give way if it is safe to do so
- sound your horn and keep going
- slow down and then sound your horn

Answer

- slow down and give way if it is safe to do so

Give way to buses whenever you can do so safely, especially when they signal to pull away from bus stops. Look out for people leaving the bus and crossing the road.

DSA THEORY TEST for motorcyclists

Question 2.18

Mark one answer

What should you use your horn for?

- To alert others to your presence
- To allow you right of way
- To greet other road users
- To signal your annoyance

Answer

■ **To alert others to your presence**

Don't use it to

- greet others
- show impatience
- give priority.

Your horn shouldn't be used between 11.30 pm and 7 am in a built-up area or when your motorcycle is stationary – unless a moving vehicle poses a danger.

Question 2.19

Mark one answer

You are in a one-way street and want to turn right. You should position yourself

- in the right-hand lane
- in the left-hand lane
- in either lane, depending on the traffic
- just left of the centre line

Answer

■ **in the right-hand lane**

If you're travelling in a one-way street and wish to turn right you should take up a position in the right-hand lane. This will enable other road users not wishing to turn to proceed on the left. Indicate your intention and take up your position in good time.

Question 2.20

Mark one answer

You wish to turn right ahead. Why should you take up the correct position in good time?

- To allow other drivers to pull out in front of you
- To give a better view into the road that you're joining
- To help other road users know what you intend to do
- To allow drivers to pass you on the right

Answer

■ **To help other road users know what you intend to do**

If you wish to turn right into a side road take up your position in good time. Move to the centre of the road when it's safe to do so. This will allow vehicles to pass you on the left. Early planning will show other traffic what you intend to do.

Mark one answer

At a puffin crossing what colour follows the green signal?

- Steady red
- Flashing amber
- Steady amber
- Flashing green

Answer

- **Steady amber**

Puffin crossings have infra-red sensors which detect when pedestrians are crossing and hold the red traffic signal until the crossing is clear. The use of a sensor means there is no flashing amber phase as there is with a pelican crossing.

Mark one answer

You are riding on a country road. Two horses with riders are in the distance. You should

- continue at your normal speed
- change down the gears quickly
- slow down and be ready to stop
- flash your headlight to warn them

Answer

- **slow down and be ready to stop**

Animals are easily frightened by moving motor vehicles. If you're approaching horses you should keep your speed down and watch to see if the rider has any difficulty keeping control. Always be ready to stop if necessary.

Mark one answer

You should never wave people across at pedestrian crossings because

- there may be another vehicle coming
- they may not be looking
- it is safer for you to carry on
- they may not be ready to cross

Answer

- **there may be another vehicle coming**

If it's safe you should always stop for pedestrians waiting at pedestrian crossings. Don't wave them to cross the road since another driver may not

- have seen them
- have seen your signal
- be able to stop safely.

Question 2.24

Mark one answer

At a pelican crossing the flashing amber light means you MUST

▪ stop and wait for the green light

▪ stop and wait for the red light

▪ give way to pedestrians waiting to cross

▪ give way to pedestrians already on the crossing

Answer

▪ **give way to pedestrians already on the crossing**

Pelican crossings are light-controlled crossings where pedestrians use push-button controls to change the signals. Pelican crossings have no red-and-amber stage before green. Instead, they have a flashing amber light, which means you must give way to pedestrians on the crossing. If it's clear, you may go on.

Question 2.25

Mark one answer

Following this vehicle too closely is unwise because

▪ your brakes will overheat

▪ your view ahead is increased

▪ your engine will overheat

▪ your view ahead is reduced

Answer

▪ **your view ahead is reduced**

Staying back will increase your view of the road ahead. This will help you to see any hazards that might occur and allow you more time to react.

Question 2.26

Mark two answers

When riding a motorcycle your normal road position should allow

- other vehicles to overtake on your left
- the driver ahead to see you in the mirrors
- you to prevent following vehicles from overtaking
- you to be seen by traffic that is emerging from junctions ahead
- you to ride within half a metre (1 foot 8 inches) of the kerb

Question 2.27

Mark one answer

You are in a line of traffic. The driver behind you is following very closely. What action should you take?

- Ignore the following driver and continue to drive within the speed limit
- Slow down, gradually increasing the gap between you and the vehicle in front
- Signal left and wave the following driver past
- Move over to a position just left of the centre line of the road

Question 2.28

Mark one answer

You are travelling at the legal speed limit. A vehicle comes up quickly behind, flashing its headlights. You should

- accelerate to make a gap behind you
- touch the brakes sharply to show your brake lights
- maintain your speed to prevent the vehicle from overtaking
- allow the vehicle to overtake

Answers

- **the driver ahead to see you in the mirrors**
- **you to be seen by traffic that is emerging from junctions ahead**

Keep clear of the centre of the road. You might

- obstruct overtaking traffic
- put yourself in danger from oncoming traffic
- encourage other traffic to overtake you on the left.

Answer

- **Slow down, gradually increasing the gap between you and the vehicle in front**

It can be worrying to see that the car behind is following you too closely. If you ease back from the vehicle in front you'll give yourself a greater safety margin.

Answer

- **allow the vehicle to overtake**

Don't enforce the speed limit by blocking another vehicle's progress. This will only lead to the other driver becoming more frustrated. Allow the other vehicle to pass when you can do so safely.

DSA THEORY TEST for motorcyclists

Question 2.29

Mark three answers

Which of the following vehicles will use blue flashing beacons?

- Motorway maintenance
- Bomb disposal
- Blood transfusion
- Police patrol
- Breakdown recovery

Answers

- **Bomb disposal**
- **Blood transfusion**
- **Police patrol**

Try to move out of the way of emergency vehicles with blue flashing beacons. Do so safely and without delay.

Question 2.30

Mark one answer

When being followed by an ambulance showing a flashing blue beacon you should

- pull over as soon as safely possible to let it pass
- accelerate hard to get away from it
- maintain your speed and course
- brake harshly and immediately stop in the road

Answer

- **pull over as soon as safely possible to let it pass**

Pull over where the ambulance can pass safely. Check that there are no bollards or obstructions in the road that will prevent it doing so.

Question 2.31

Mark one answer

What type of emergency vehicle is fitted with a green flashing beacon?

- Fire engine
- Road gritter
- Ambulance
- Doctor's car

Answer

- **Doctor's car**

A green flashing beacon on a vehicle means the driver or passenger is a doctor on an emergency call. Give way to them if it's safe to do so. Be aware that the vehicle may be travelling quickly or may stop in a hurry.

Mark one answer

A vehicle has a flashing green beacon. What does this mean?

- A doctor is answering an emergency call
- The vehicle is slow-moving
- It is a motorway police patrol vehicle
- A vehicle is carrying hazardous chemicals

Answer

- **A doctor is answering an emergency call**

A doctor attending an emergency might show a green flashing beacon on his or her vehicle. Give way to them as they will need to reach their destination quickly. Be aware that they might pull over suddenly.

Mark one answer

At which type of crossing are cyclists allowed to ride across with pedestrians?

- Toucan
- Puffin
- Pelican
- Zebra

Answer

- **Toucan**

A Toucan crossing is designed to allow pedestrians and cyclists to cross at the same time. Be prepared to look out for fast approaching cyclists.

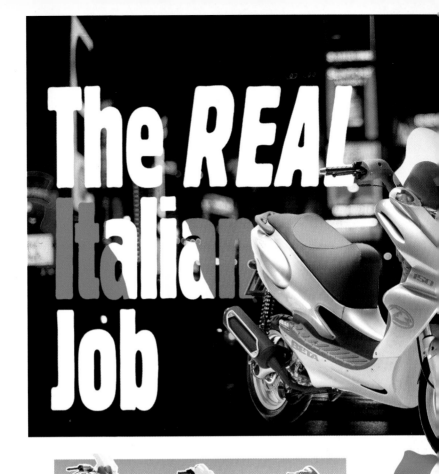

The REAL Italian Job

a series starts @ £1840 otr
ble in 50cc, 125cc and 150cc

Ark series starts @ £1590 otr
50cc air cooled in yellow and black
Also in 50cc liquid cooled

Quadra @ £1490
Available in blue and

rmoto starts @ £1989 otr
ble in 50cc and 72cc - road tyres

T starts @ £2890 otr
Available in 125cc and 200cc black or red

Beta offer a fantastic choice of designer bikes and

scooters. They will take you into the world of

motorcycling in the most enjoyable way possible.

Whether it's street, commuter, sports or cruising.

There's something for all tastes.

For a piece of Italian action contact

020 8665 9994

This section looks at safety and your motorcycle.

The questions will ask you about

- **Fault detection**

  be able to detect minor faults on your motorcycle

- **Defects and their effects on safety**

  be aware that an unroadworthy motorcycle might endanger your pillion passenger or other road users.

- **Use of safety equipment**

  make sure you have any necessary training

- **Emissions**

  make sure your motorcycle complies with correct emissions regulations.

- **Noise**

  make sure that your motorcycle is not too noisy. Prevent excessive noise, especially at night.

Mark one answer

When riding a different motorcycle you should

- ask someone to ride with you for the first time
- ride as soon as possible as all controls and switches are the same
- leave your gloves behind so switches can be operated easier at first
- be sure you know where all controls and switches are

Answer

- **be sure you know where all controls and switches are**

Before you ride any motorcycle make sure you're familiar with the layout of all the controls and switches. While control layouts are generally similar, there may be differences in their feel and method of operation.

Question 3.2

Mark one answer

When should you especially check the engine oil level?

- Before a long journey
- When the engine is hot
- Early in the morning
- Every 6000 miles

Answer
- **Before a long journey**

Also make checks on

- fuel
- water
- tyres.

Question 3.3

Mark one answer

Which of these, if allowed to get low, could cause an accident?

- Antifreeze level
- Brake fluid level
- Battery water level
- Radiator coolant level

Answer
- **Brake fluid level**

In order to keep your machine in good working order you should carry out frequent checks. As a rider you must ensure that you're using a safe machine that won't endanger other road users.

Mark one answer

A loose drive chain on a motorcycle could cause

- the front wheel to wobble
- the ignition to cut out
- the brakes to fail
- the rear wheel to lock

Answer

- **the rear wheel to lock**

Drive chains are subject to wear and require frequent adjustment and lubrication. If the chain is worn or slack it can jump off the sprocket and lock the rear wheel.

Question 3.5

Mark three answers

A wrongly adjusted drive chain can

- cause an accident
- make wheels wobble
- create a noisy rattle
- affect gear changing
- cause a suspension fault

Answers

- **cause an accident**
- **create a noisy rattle**
- **affect gear changing**

A motorcycle drive chain will stretch as it wears and needs adjusting to keep the tension correct. If the chain is wrongly adjusted it can

- jump off the sprocket and lock the rear wheel causing loss of control
- rattle as it flaps loosely
- cause problems selecting gears.

Question 3.6

Mark two answers

Which TWO are badly affected if the tyres are under-inflated?

- Braking
- Steering
- Changing gear
- Parking

Answers

- **Braking**
- **Steering**

Your tyres are your only contact with the road and therefore very important to your safety. Incorrect tyre pressures will affect steering and braking, so it's very important that you take the time to attend to them. Correct tyre pressures can reduce the risk of skidding and will provide a more comfortable ride.

Question 3.7

Mark one answer

What is the most important reason why you should keep your motorcycle regularly maintained?

- To accelerate faster than other traffic
- So the motorcycle can carry panniers
- To keep the motorcycle roadworthy
- So the motorcycle can carry a passenger

Answer

■ **To keep the motorcycle roadworthy**

Whenever you use any motorcycle on the road it must be in a roadworthy condition. Regular maintenance will help to identify any faults at an early stage and help avoid more serious problems.

Question 3.8

Mark one answer

It is essential that tyre pressures are checked regularly. When should this be done?

- After any lengthy journey
- After travelling at high speed
- When tyres are hot
- When tyres are cold

Answer

■ **When tyres are cold**

When you check the tyre pressures do so when the tyres are cold. This will give you a more accurate reading. The heat generated from a long journey will raise the pressure inside the tyre.

Question 3.9

Mark one answer

How often should motorcycle tyre pressures be checked?

- Only during each regular service
- After each long journey
- At least monthly
- At least weekly

Answer

■ **At least weekly**

As a motorcyclist your tyres are vital to your safety. Make sure that you check the pressure in your tyres at least once a week. Don't ride your motorcycle if the tyres are incorrectly inflated.

Question 3.10

Mark one answer

The legal minimum depth of tread for motorcycle tyres is

- 1 mm
- 1.6 mm
- 2.5 mm
- 4 mm

Answer

- **1 mm**

The entire original tread should be continuous. Don't ride a motorcycle with worn tyres.

Your tyres are your only contact with the road so it's very important that you ensure they're in good condition.

Question 3.11

Mark one answer

Your motorcycle has tubed tyres fitted as standard. When replacing a tyre you should

- replace the tube if it is 6 months old
- replace the tube if it has covered 6,000 miles
- replace the tube only if replacing the rear tyre
- replace the tube with each change of tyre

Answer

- **replace the tube with each change of tyre**

It isn't worth taking risks to save money. Your life could depend on the condition of your motorcycle.

Question 3.12

Mark four answers

You are riding a motorcycle of more than 50 cc. Which FOUR would make a tyre illegal?

- Tread less than 1.6 mm deep
- Tread less than 1 mm deep
- A large bulge in the wall
- A recut tread
- Exposed ply or cord
- A stone wedged in the tread

Answers

- **Tread less than 1 mm deep**
- **A large bulge in the wall**
- **A recut tread**
- **Exposed ply or cord**

When checking tyres make sure there are no bulges or cuts in the side walls. Always buy your tyres from a reputable dealer to ensure quality and value for money.

Question 3.13

Mark one answer

How should you ride a motorcycle when NEW tyres have just been fitted?

- Carefully, until the shiny surface is worn off
- By braking hard especially into bends
- Through normal riding with higher air pressures
- By riding at faster than normal speeds

Answer

- **Carefully, until the shiny surface is worn off**

New tyres have a shiny finish which needs to be worn off before the tyre will give the best grip, especially if the roads are wet.

Question 3.14

Mark two answers

You should maintain cable operated brakes

- by regular adjustment when necessary
- at normal service times only
- yearly, before taking the motorcycle for its MoT
- by oiling cables and pivots regularly

Answers

- **by regular adjustment when necessary**
- **by oiling cables and pivots regularly**

Keeping your brakes in good working order is vital for road safety. With cable operated brakes the cables need

- adjustment because they will stretch with use
- lubrication to prevent friction and wear of the cables and pivots.

Question 3.15

Mark one answer

When MUST you use dipped headlights during the day?

- All the time
- Along narrow streets
- In poor visibility
- When parking

Answer

- **In poor visibility**

This will allow other road users to see you. You should use them in heavy rain, mist, or in foggy conditions.

Question 3.16

Mark three answers

Motor vehicles can harm the environment. This has resulted in

- air pollution
- damage to buildings
- reduced health risks
- improved public transport
- less use of electrical vehicles
- using up natural resources

Answers

- air pollution
- damage to buildings
- using up natural resources

Exhaust emissions cause buildings to discolour and erode. Millions of pounds have been spent restoring old buildings to their original state. Constant vibration caused by heavy traffic also damages buildings.

Question 3.17

Mark three answers

To reduce the damage your motorcycle causes to the environment you should

- use narrow side streets
- avoid harsh acceleration
- brake in good time
- anticipate well ahead
- use busy routes

Answers

- avoid harsh acceleration
- brake in good time
- anticipate well ahead

By looking well ahead and recognising hazards early you can avoid last minute harsh braking. Watch the traffic flow and judge your speed accordingly. Avoid over revving the engine and accelerating harshly.

Question 3.18

Mark one answer

Which of the following would NOT make you more visible in daylight?

- A black helmet
- A white helmet
- Switching on your dipped headlamp
- Wearing a fluorescent jacket

Answer

- A black helmet

Wearing bright or fluorescent clothes will help other road users to see you. Wearing a white helmet can also make you more visible.

Question 3.19

Mark one answer

When riding and wearing brightly coloured clothing you will

dazzle other motorists on the road

be seen more easily by other motorists

create a hazard by distracting other drivers

be able to ride on unlit roads at night with sidelights

Answer

be seen more easily by other motorists

For safety you want other road users to see you easily. One way of achieving this is to wear brightly coloured or fluorescent clothing during daylight. At night reflective clothing is the best material to help others to see you.

Reflective

Reflective

Question 3.20

Mark one answer

You are riding a motorcycle in very hot weather. You should

ride with your visor fully open

continue to wear protective clothing

wear trainers instead of boots

slacken your helmet strap

Answer

continue to wear protective clothing

In very hot weather it's tempting to ride in light summer clothes. Don't do this. If you fall from your motorcycle you'll have no protection from the hard road surface. Always wear your protective clothing, whatever the weather.

Mark one answer

Why should you wear fluorescent clothing when riding in daylight?

- It reduces wind resistance
- It prevents injury if you come off the machine
- It helps other road users to see you
- It keeps you cool in hot weather

Answer

■ **It helps other road users to see you**

When riding a motorcycle it's very important that other road users are able to see you clearly. Fluorescent clothing will help towards this, reducing the risk of an accident. You must be visible from all sides.

Question 3.22

Mark one answer

Why should riders wear reflective clothing?

- To protect them from the cold
- To protect them from direct sunlight
- To be seen better in daylight
- To be seen better at night

Answer

■ **To be seen better at night**

Fluorescent clothing will help others to see you during the day. At night, however, you should wear clothing that reflects the light. This allows other road users to see you with their headlights. Ask your local motorcycle dealer about the correct clothing.

Question 3.23

Mark three answers

Which of the following make it easier for motorcyclists to be seen?

- Using a dipped headlight
- Wearing a fluorescent jacket
- Wearing a white helmet
- Wearing a grey helmet
- Wearing black leathers
- Using a tinted visor

Answers

■ **Using a dipped headlight**

■ **Wearing a fluorescent jacket**

■ **Wearing a white helmet**

Many road accidents involving motorcyclists occur because another road user didn't see them. Using some form of visibility aid will help others to see you. Be aware that you're vulnerable and ride defensively.

DSA THEORY TEST for motorcyclists

Question 3.24

Mark three answers

Excessive or uneven tyre wear can be caused by faults in which THREE?

- The gearbox
- The braking system
- The accelerator
- The exhaust system
- Wheel alignment
- The suspension

Answers

- **The braking system**
- **Wheel alignment**
- **The suspension**

Regular servicing will help to detect faults at an early stage and help prevent minor faults becoming serious or even dangerous.

Question 3.25

Mark one answer

Which of the following fairings would give you the best weather protection?

- Handlebar
- Sports
- Touring
- Windscreen

Answer

- **Touring**

Fairings give protection to the hands, legs and feet. They also make riding more comfortable by keeping you out of the wind

Question 3.26

Mark one answer

It would be illegal to ride WITH a helmet on when

- the helmet is not fastened correctly
- the helmet is more than four years old
- you have borrowed someone else's helmet
- the helmet does not have chin protection

Answer

- **the helmet is not fastened correctly**

In an accident a motorcycle helmet which is incorrectly fastened is liable to come off and provide little or no protection. The law requires that when you ride on the road your helmet must be correctly fastened.

Question 3.27

Mark one answer

Your safety helmet has a small crack. You should

- get a new one before riding
- ride at low speeds only
- ask the police to inspect it
- have it repaired by an expert

Answer

☐ **get a new one before riding**

If you damage your motorcycle helmet, even slightly, buy a new one. The smallest damage can make a helmet unreliable. A little expense now may save your life later.

Buy a white helmet if possible. They're much more easily seen by other road users.

Question 3.28

Mark one answer

Your visor becomes badly scratched. You should

- polish it with a fine abrasive
- replace it
- wash it in soapy water
- clean it with petrol

Answer

☐ **replace it**

Your visor protects your eyes from wind, rain, insects and road dirt. It's therefore important to keep it clean and in good repair. A badly scratched visor might

- obscure your view
- cause dazzle from lights of oncoming vehicles.

Question 3.29

Mark two answers

You want to ride your motorcycle in the dark. What could you wear to be seen more easily?

- A black leather jacket
- Reflective clothing
- A white helmet
- A red helmet

Answers

☐ **Reflective clothing**

☐ **A white helmet**

When riding in the dark you will be more easy to see if you wear

- reflective clothing
- a white helmet.

A white helmet contrasts starkly with the surrounding darkness, while reflective clothing reflects the light from other vehicles and makes the rider much more visible.

Question 3.30

Mark one answer

You must NOT sound your horn

- between 10 pm and 6 am in a built-up area
- at any time in a built-up area
- between 11.30 pm and 7 am in a built-up area
- between 11.30 pm and 6 am on any road

Answer

- **between 11.30 pm and 7 am in a built-up area**

Vehicles can be noisy. Every effort must be made to prevent excessive noise, especially in built-up areas at night. Don't

- rev the engine
- sound the horn between 11.30 pm and 7 am.

Question 3.31

Mark one answer

When should you NOT use your horn in a built-up area?

- Between 8 pm and 8 am
- Between 9 pm and dawn
- Between dusk and 8 am
- Between 11.30 pm and 7 am

Answer

- **Between 11.30 pm and 7 am**

Flash your headlights as an alternative. Only sound your horn to prevent an accident.

Question 3.32

Mark one answer

Why are mirrors often slightly curved (convex)?

- They give a wider field of vision
- They totally cover blind spots
- They make it easier to judge the speed of following traffic
- They make following traffic look bigger

Answer

- **They give a wider field of vision**

Modern vehicles provide the driver with the equipment to help increase the field of vision. However, you should always be aware that even these mirrors might not reflect all that is around the vehicle. A check over the shoulder before you move off will be required.

Mark one answer

Why can it be helpful to have mirrors fitted on each side of your motorcycle?

- To judge the gap when filtering in traffic
- To give protection when riding in poor weather
- To make your motorcycle appear larger to other drivers
- To give you the best view of the road behind

Answer

■ **To give you the best view of the road behind**

When riding on the road you need to know as much about following traffic as you can. A mirror fitted on each side of your motorcycle will help give you the best view of the road behind.

Mark one answer

When MUST you use a dipped headlight during the day?

- On country roads
- In poor visibility
- Along narrow streets
- When parking

Answer

■ **In poor visibility**

It's important that other road users can see you clearly at all times. It will help them to see you if you use a dipped headlight during the day. If there's limited visibility you MUST do so.

Mark one answer

Your side stand is not raised fully when you start to ride. What could this do?

- Alter the motorcycle's centre of gravity
- Catch on your feet
- Dig into the ground when you are cornering
- Cause the motorcycle to steer badly

Answer

■ **Dig into the ground when you are cornering**

Make sure that your side stand is fully up before you move off. If it isn't up it could dig into the ground as you move away and might lead to an accident.

Question 3.36

Mark one answer

What is most likely to cause high fuel consumption?

- Poor steering control
- Accelerating around bends
- Staying in high gears
- Harsh braking and accelerating

Answer

■ **Harsh braking and accelerating**

Look after your motorcycle. Have it regularly serviced and keep all the lights and any screen clean. Riding 'sympathetically' will help you to keep fuel consumption down. This practice is kinder to the environment and will also save you money.

Question 3.37

Mark two answers

A properly serviced motorcycle will give

- lower insurance premiums
- you a refund on your road tax
- better fuel economy
- cleaner exhaust emissions

Answers

■ **better fuel economy**

■ **cleaner exhaust emissions**

When you purchase your motorcycle, check at what intervals you should have it serviced. This can vary depending on model or manufacturer. Use the service manual and keep it up to date. The cleaner the engine, the cleaner it's emissions.

Question 3.38

Mark three answers

The pictured vehicle is 'environmentally friendly' because it

- reduces noise pollution
- uses diesel fuel
- uses electricity
- uses unleaded fuel
- reduces parking spaces
- reduces town traffic

Answers

■ **reduces noise pollution**

■ **uses electricity**

■ **reduces town traffic**

The electric motors of trams don't emit dirty fumes which would add to those already emitted by the other town traffic. This type of motor is also much quieter than petrol or diesel engines.

Mark one answer

Supertrams or Light Rapid Transit (LRT) systems are environmentally friendly because

◻ they use diesel power

◻ they use quieter roads

◻ they use electric power

◻ they do not operate during rush hour

Answer

◻ **they use electric power**

This means that they do not emit toxic fumes, adding to city pollution problems. They are also a lot quieter and smoother to ride on.

Mark one answer

'Red routes' in major cities have been introduced to

◻ raise the speed limits

◻ help the traffic flow

◻ provide better parking

◻ allow lorries to load more freely

Answer

◻ **help the traffic flow**

Traffic jams today are often caused by the volume of traffic. However, selfish parking can lead to the closure of an inside lane, and traffic having to wait for oncoming vehicles, can also cause delays. All the time the traffic is moving slowly, each engine is emitting toxic fumes.

Mark one answer

In some narrow residential streets you will find a speed limit of

◻ 20 mph

◻ 25 mph

◻ 35 mph

◻ 40 mph

Answer

◻ **20 mph**

There are numerous hazards to deal with in residential areas. These hazards can be unpredictable, hidden, static or moving. You need to allow yourself the time and space to deal with them. The safest way to do this is to reduce your speed.

Question 3.42

Mark one answer

Road humps, chicanes, and narrowings are

- always at major road works
- used to increase traffic speed
- at toll-bridge approaches only
- traffic calming measures

Question 3.43

Mark one answer

You enter a road where there are road humps. What should you do?

- Maintain a reduced speed throughout
- Accelerate quickly between each one
- Always keep to the maximum legal speed
- Ride slowly at school times only

Answer

■ **traffic calming measures**

Remember that the motorcycle is a relatively late addition to our environment. Many areas, especially residential ones, were not built to allow for fast moving traffic. Measures are now being taken to slow traffic down.

Answer

■ **Maintain a reduced speed throughout**

The humps are there for a reason: to reduce the speed of the traffic. Don't accelerate harshly between them as this means you will only have to brake harshly to negotiate the next hump. Harsh braking and acceleration use more fuel.

Question 3.44

Mark three answers

A motorcyclist may only carry a pillion passenger when

- [ ] the rider has successfully completed CBT (Compulsory Basic Training)
- [ ] the rider holds a full licence for the category of motorcycle
- [ ] the motorcycle is fitted with rear foot pegs
- [ ] the rider has a full car licence and is over 21
- [ ] there is a proper passenger seat fitted
- [ ] there is no sidecar fitted to the machine

Answers

- the rider holds a full licence for the category of motorcycle
- the motorcycle is fitted with rear foot pegs
- there is a proper passenger seat fitted

Before carrying a passenger on a motorcycle the rider must hold a full licence for the category being ridden and make sure that

- passenger footrests are fitted
- a proper passenger seat is fitted.

Question 3.45

Mark two answers

For which TWO of these may you use hazard warning lights?

- [ ] When travelling on a motorway, to warn drivers behind of a hazard ahead
- [ ] When you are double parked on a two-way road
- [ ] When your direction indicators are not working
- [ ] When warning oncoming traffic that you intend to stop
- [ ] When your motorcycle has broken down and is causing an obstruction

Answers

- When travelling on a motorway, to warn drivers behind of a hazard ahead
- When your vehicle has broken down and is causing an obstruction

Don't use them as an excuse to park illegally, such as when using a cash machine or postbox. They are an important safety feature and should only be used to warn other road users of a hazard.

Question 3.46

Mark one answer

Tyre pressures should be increased on your motorcycle when

- [ ] riding on a wet road
- [ ] carrying a pillion passenger
- [ ] travelling on an uneven surface
- [ ] riding on twisty roads

Answer

- carrying a pillion passenger

Sometimes manufacturers advise you to increase your tyre pressures for high speed riding and when carrying extra weight.

This information can be found in the handbook.

Question 3.47

Mark one answer

Your oil light comes on as you are riding. You should

☐ go to a dealer for an oil change

☐ go to the nearest garage for their advice

☐ ride slowly for a few miles to see if the light goes out

☐ stop as quickly as possible and try to find the cause

Answer

☐ **stop as quickly as possible and try to find the cause**

If the oil pressure warning light comes on when the engine is running you may have a serious problem. Do NOT continue riding.

Question 3.48

Mark three answers

When may you have to increase the tyre pressures on your motorcycle?

☐ When carrying a pillion passenger

☐ After a long journey

☐ When carrying heavy loads

☐ When riding at high speeds

☐ When riding in hot weather

Answers

☐ **When carrying a pillion passenger**

☐ **When carrying heavy loads**

☐ **When riding at high speeds**

Read the manufacturer's handbook to see if they recommend increasing tyre pressures under certain conditions.

Question 3.49

Mark two answers

Which TWO of these items on a motorcycle MUST be kept clean?

☐ Number plate

☐ Wheels

☐ Engine

☐ Fairing

☐ Headlights

Answers

☐ **Number plate**

☐ **Headlights**

Maintenance is a vital part of road safety. Lights, indicators, reflectors and number plates MUST be kept clean and clear.

Mark two answers

Motorcycle tyres MUST

- [ ] have the same tread pattern
- [ ] be correctly inflated
- [ ] be the same size, front and rear
- [ ] both be the same make
- [ ] have sufficient tread depth

Answers

- [ ] **be correctly inflated**
- [ ] **have sufficient tread depth**

Your safety and that of others may depend on the condition of your tyres. Before you ride you must check they are correctly inflated and have sufficient tread depth. Make sure these checks become part of a routine.

Question 3.51

Mark one answer

You are riding on a wet road. When braking you should

- [ ] apply the rear brake well before the front
- [ ] apply the front brake just before the rear
- [ ] avoid using the front brake at all
- [ ] avoid using the rear brake at all

Answer

- [ ] **apply the front brake just before the rear**

On wet roads you will have to be especially careful, brake earlier and more smoothly. Try to brake when the motorcycle is upright.

Question 3.52

Mark one answer

You should use the engine cut-out switch on your motorcycle to

- [ ] save wear and tear on the battery
- [ ] stop the engine on short stops
- [ ] stop the engine in an emergency
- [ ] save wear and tear on the ignition

Answer

- [ ] **stop the engine in an emergency**

When stopping the engine normally, use the ignition switch.

Question 3.53

Mark one answer

Riding your motorcycle with a slack or worn drive chain may cause

- an engine misfire
- early tyre wear
- increased emissions
- a locked wheel

Answer

■ **a locked wheel**

Check your drive chain regularly and adjust it if necessary. (chains need frequent adjustment and lubrication.) It needs to be adjusted until the free play is as specified in the handbook. Always use a special chain lubricant.

Question 3.54

Mark one answer

You have adjusted the drive chain tension. You should check the

- rear wheel alignment
- tyre pressures
- valve clearances
- sidelights

Answer

■ **rear wheel alignment**

Drive chains wear and need frequent adjustment and lubrication. If the drive chain is worn or slack it can jump off the sprocket and lock the rear wheel.

When you have adjusted the chain tension, you need to check the rear wheel alignment. Marks by the chain adjusters may be provided to make this easier.

Question 3.55

Mark one answer

You will use more fuel if you ride your motorcycle with tyres that are

- under-inflated
- of different makes
- over-inflated
- new and hardly used

Answer

■ **under-inflated**

Check your tyre pressures frequently – normally once a week. If pressures are lower than those recommended by the manufacturer there will be more 'rolling resistance' and the engine will have to work harder to overcome this.

Question 3.56

Mark two answers

How should you dispose of a used motorcycle battery?

- [ ] Take it to a local authority site
- [ ] Put it in the dustbin
- [ ] Break it up into pieces
- [ ] Leave it on waste land
- [ ] Take it to a garage
- [ ] Burn it on a fire

Answers

- ▪ **Take it to a local authority site**
- ▪ **Take it to a garage**

Old batteries contain acid and can cause pollution. They should be disposed of safely.

Question 3.57

Mark one answer

The purpose of a catalytic converter is to reduce

- [ ] fuel consumption
- [ ] the risk of fire
- [ ] toxic exhaust gases
- [ ] engine wear

Answer

- ▪ **toxic exhaust gases**

Catalytic converters are designed to reduce toxic emissions by up to 90 per cent. They work more efficiently when the engine has reached its normal working temperature.

Question 3.58

Mark one answer

Which of these fuels should be used in a motorcycle fitted with a catalytic converter?

- [ ] Leaded petrol
- [ ] Propane gas
- [ ] Butane gas
- [ ] Unleaded petrol

Answer

- ▪ **Unleaded petrol**

If used in a motorcycle fitted with a catalytic converter, leaded petrol will damage the specially treated filter inside the unit.

Question 3.59

Mark one answer

Your motorcycle has a catalytic converter. Its purpose is to reduce

- exhaust noise
- fuel consumption
- exhaust emissions
- engine noise

Answer

exhaust emissions

Catalytic converters reduce the harmful gases given out by the engine. These gases are changed by a chemical process as they pass through a specially treated honeycomb filter.

Question 3.60

Mark one answer

Catalytic converters are fitted to make the

- engine produce more power
- exhaust system easier to replace
- engine run quietly
- exhaust fumes cleaner

Answer

exhaust fumes cleaner

Harmful gases in the exhaust system pollute the atmosphere. These gases are reduced by up to 90 per cent if a catalytic converter is fitted. These converters can be especially beneficial to those of us who live and work near congested roads.

You've made one good decision...

Now make another

MAG IS BRITAIN'S LEADING RIDERS ORGANISATION

- Specialist insurance deals: **MAG Direct**

- Numerous **discounts** with product and service providers

- **Breakdown Service**

- **Nationwide** Social Scene and Runs/Rallies

- **StreetBiker** ~ The **best** motorcycle paper in print ~ delivered FREE to your door.

- **Your** interests politically represented at all levels ~ locally in Westminster and Brussels

ANNUAL SUBS £20

Membership by cred card or write to:

MAG UK
PO BOX 750
Rugby
CV21 3ZR

Telephone
0870 444 8448

Facsimile
0870 444 8449

or visit
www.mag-uk.org

MOTORCYCLE ACTION GROUP

HORIZON

Motorcycle Training

- C.B.T.
- Direct Access
- Full Licence Course
- D.S.A. Approved
- BMF Blue Riband
- Advanced Training
- Instructor Training

Tel: 01908 694333
Tel: 01865 778877
Tel: 01295 265656
Tel: 01604 752020
Fax: 01908 225766

PERSONAL TUITION

Horizon Motorcycle Training policy of giving a professional, friendly service at a 'value for money price' means small training groups.

However we can offer personal tuition with or without motorcycle hire on a hourly rate basis – times to suit client.

7 Days a Week

PO Box 3057, Dawson Road, Milton Keynes, MK7 8ZG
Sites at Oxford, Milton Keynes, Banbury & Northampton
Visit us at://website.lineone.net/~hmct/
e-mail: hmct@lineone.net

This section looks at safety margins and how they can be affected by conditions.

The questions will ask you about

- **Stopping distances**

  leave enough room to stop in all conditions.

- **Road surfaces**

  be aware of uneven or slippery surfaces.

- **Skidding**

  be aware that preventing a skid is most important, but you should also know how to react should you lose control of your motorcycle.

- **Weather conditions**

  be aware that weather conditions will have an effect on how your motorcycle behaves.

Question 4.1

Mark one answer

You are on a good, dry road surface and your motorcycle has good brakes and tyres. What is the overall stopping distance at 40 mph?

■ 23 metres (75 feet)
■ 36 metres (118 feet)
■ 53 metres (175 feet)
■ 96 metres (315 feet)

Answer

■ **36 metres (118 feet)**

Factors that affect how long it takes you to stop include

- how fast you're going
- whether you're travelling on the level, uphill or downhill
- the weather and road conditions
- the condition of tyres, brakes and suspension
- your reaction times.

Question 4.2

Mark one answer

You are on a good, dry road surface. Your motorcycle has good brakes and tyres. What is the braking distance at 50 mph?

■ 38 metres (125 feet)
■ 14 metres (46 feet)
■ 24 metres (79 feet)
■ 55 metres (180 feet)

Answer

■ **38 metres (125 feet)**

Stopping distance can be divided into

- thinking distance
- braking distance.

The thinking distance is how far you travel from the moment you see the need to brake to the moment you apply the brakes.

The braking distance is how far you travel from the moment you first apply the brakes to the point where you stop.

Question 4.3

Mark one answer

Your overall stopping distance will be longer when riding

■ at night
■ in the fog
■ with a passenger
■ up a hill

Answer

■ **with a passenger**

When carrying a passenger on a motorcycle the overall weight will be much more than when riding alone. This additional weight will make it harder for you to stop in an emergency.

Mark one answer

You are riding a motorcycle in good road conditions. The most effective way to use the brakes is to

◻ apply both brakes with greater pressure on the rear

◻ apply both brakes with equal pressure

◻ apply the rear brake first and the front just before you stop

◻ apply both brakes with greater pressure on the front

Answer

◻ **apply both brakes with greater pressure on the front**

This technique gives the best stopping power in good conditions because

• the combined weight of the motorcycle and rider is thrown forward

• the front tyre is pressed more firmly on the road, giving a better grip.

Question 4.5

Mark one answer

What is the shortest stopping distance at 70 mph?

◻ 53 metres (175 feet)

◻ 60 metres (197 feet)

◻ 73 metres (240 feet)

◻ 96 metres (315 feet)

Answer

◻ **96 metres (315 feet)**

Note that this is the *shortest* distance. It will take *at least* this distance to think, brake and stop.

Typical Stopping Distances

Typical Stopping Distances

20 mph — = 12 metres (40 feet) or 3 car lengths — 6 metres / 6 metres

30 mph — = 23 metres (75 feet) or 6 car lengths — 9 metres / 14 metres

40 mph — = 36 metres (120 feet) or 9 car lengths — 12 metres / 24 metres

50 mph — = 53 metres (175 feet) or 13 car lengths — 15 metres / 38 metres

60 mph — = 73 metres (240 feet) or 18 car lengths — 18 metres / 55 metres

70 mph — = 96 metres (315 feet) or 24 car lengths — 21 metres / 75 metres

■ Thinking Distance

■ Braking Distance

average car length = 4 metres

GiVi

info@givi.co.uk
www.givi.co.uk

movement is
energy

GiVi Concessionaires Ltd
Unit 4 • Royal Oak Court
Royal Oak Way
• Royal Oak Industrial Estate
Daventry • Northants NN11 5PQ
Tel: (01327) 706220
• Fax: (01327) 706239
email: info@givi.co.uk

Question 4.6

Mark one answer

What is the shortest overall stopping distance on a dry road from 60 mph?

- 53 metres (175 feet)
- 58 metres (190 feet)
- 73 metres (240 feet)
- 96 metres (315 feet)

Answer

73 metres (240 feet)

Pace out 73 metres and then look back. It's probably further than you think.

Question 4.7

Mark one answer

'Only a fool breaks the Two-Second Rule' refers to

- the time recommended when using the choke
- the separation distance when riding in good conditions
- restarting a stalled engine in busy traffic
- the time you should keep your foot down at a junction

Answer

the separation distance when riding in good conditions

It is very important that you always leave a safe gap between yourself and any vehicle you're following. In good conditions you need to leave

- at least one metre for every mile per hour of your speed, or
- a two-second time interval.

Question 4.8

Mark one answer

Your overall stopping distance will be much longer when travelling

- in the rain
- in fog
- at night
- in strong winds

Answer

in the rain

Extra care should be taken in wet weather. Wet roads will affect the time it takes you to stop. Your stopping distance could be at least doubled.

Mark one answer

On a wet road what is the safest way to stop?

- Change gear without braking
- Use the back brake only
- Use the front brake only
- Use both brakes

Answer

■ **Use both brakes**

Motorcyclists need to take extra care when stopping on wet road surfaces. Plan well ahead so that you're able to brake in good time. You should

- ensure your motorcycle is upright
- brake when travelling in a straight line.

Mark one answer

The road surface is very important to motorcyclists because

- there can be many areas where road markings are poor
- some roads are tarmac and others concrete
- as traffic increases there is less room for riders
- only a small part of the tyre touches the road

Answer

■ **only a small part of the tyre touches the road**

A motorcyclist needs to be aware of the affect road conditions have on stability, steering and braking. Only a small part of the tyre is in contact with the road at any time, which means that any change to the road surface can affect the grip on the road.

Question 4.11

Mark four answers

Road surface is very important to motorcyclists. Which FOUR of these are more likely to reduce the stability of your motorcycle?

- Potholes
- Drain covers
- Concrete
- Oil patches
- Tarmac
- Loose gravel

Answers

- Potholes
- Drain covers
- Oil patches
- Loose gravel

Apart from the weather conditions, the road surface and any changes in it can affect the stability of your motorcycle. Be on the lookout for poor road surfaces.

Question 4.12

Mark one answer

You are riding in town at night. The roads are wet after rain. The reflections from wet surfaces will

- affect your stopping distance
- affect your road holding
- make it easy to see unlit objects
- make it hard to see unlit objects

Answer

- make it hard to see unlit objects

If you can't see clearly, slow down and stop. Make sure that your visor or goggles are clean.

Be extra cautious in these conditions.

Mark one answer

You are riding in heavy rain when your rear wheel skids as you accelerate. To get control again you must

- change down to a lower gear
- ease off the throttle
- brake to reduce speed
- put your feet down

Answer

- **ease off the throttle**

If you feel your back wheel beginning to skid as you pull away, ease off the throttle. This will give your rear tyre the chance to grip the road and stop the skid.

Bike skidding to the left

Direction of steering to correct skid

• **Ease off throttle**

Mark one answer

Braking distances on ice can be

- twice the normal distance
- five times the normal distance
- seven times the normal distance
- ten times the normal distance

Answer

- **ten times the normal distance**

Braking and stopping distances will also be affected by icy and snowy weather. You need to take extra care and expect your stopping distance to increase by up to ten times the normal distance.

Question 4.15

Mark one answer

Freezing conditions will affect the distance it takes you to come to a stop. You should expect stopping distances to increase by up to

- two times
- three times
- five times
- ten times

Answer

■ **ten times**

You must take the road and weather conditions into account when riding. It will take considerably longer to stop in bad weather.

Question 4.16

Mark one answer

It is snowing. Before starting your journey you should

- think if you need to ride at all
- try to avoid taking a passenger
- plan a route avoiding towns
- take a hot drink before setting out

Answer

■ **think if you need to ride at all**

Snow is one weather condition when it's better not to ride at all. If you must go out try and keep to main roads which are the most likely to be clear and well gritted.

Question 4.17

Mark one answer

When riding in extremely cold conditions what can you do to keep warm?

- Stay close to the vehicles in front
- Wear suitable clothing
- Lie flat on the tank
- Put one hand on the exhaust pipe

Answer

■ **Wear suitable clothing**

Motorcyclists are exposed to the elements and can become very cold when riding in wintry conditions. It's important to keep warm or concentration can be affected.

The only way to stay warm is to wear suitable clothing. If you do find yourself getting cold, stop at a suitable place to warm up.

Question 4.18

Mark one answer

Why should you ride with a dipped headlight on in the daytime?

- It helps other road users to see you
- It means that you can ride faster
- Other vehicles will get out of the way
- So that it is already on when it gets dark

Answer

- It helps other road users to see you

Your life could depend on being seen clearly.

Question 4.19

Mark one answer

Motorcyclists are only allowed to use high-intensity rear fog lights when

- a pillion passenger is being carried
- they ride a large touring machine
- visibility is 100 metres (328 feet) or less
- they are riding on the road for the first time

Answer

- visibility is 100 metres (328 feet) or less

If your motorcycle is fitted with high-intensity rear fog lamps you should only use them when visibility is 100 metres (328 feet) or less. This rule applies to all other motor vehicles using these lamps

Question 4.20

Mark two answers

In very hot weather the road surface can get soft. Which TWO of the following will be affected most?

- The suspension
- The steering
- The braking
- The exhaust

Answers

- The steering
- The braking

Take care when braking or cornering. Tyres don't grip well on soft tarmac.

DSA THEORY TEST for motorcyclists

Question 4.21

Mark two answers

In very hot weather the road surface can get soft. Which TWO of the following will be affected most?

- The suspension
- The grip of the tyres
- The braking
- The exhaust

Answers

- The grip of the tyres
- The braking

Only a small part of your tyres are in contact with the road. This is why you must consider and respect the surface you're on.

Question 4.22

Mark two answers

You are riding in very hot weather. What are TWO effects that melting tar has on the control of your motorcycle?

- It can make the surface slippery
- It can reduce tyre grip
- It can reduce stopping distances
- It can improve braking efficiency

Answers

- It can make the surface slippery
- It can reduce tyre grip

In hot weather never be tempted to ride without protective clothing. If you fall from your motorcycle you'll have no protection from the road surface.

Question 4.23

Mark one answer

Where are you most likely to be affected by a sidewind?

- On a narrow country lane
- On an open stretch of road
- On a busy stretch of road
- On a long, straight road

Answer

- On an open stretch of road

In windy conditions care must be taken on exposed roads. A strong gust of wind can blow you off course.

Question 4.24

Mark one answer

In windy conditions you need to take extra care when

▪ using the brakes

▪ making a hill start

▪ turning into a narrow road

▪ passing pedal cyclists

Answer

▪ **passing pedal cyclists**

You should always give cyclists plenty of room when overtaking. When it's windy a sudden gust could blow them off course.

Question 4.25

Mark one answer

Your indicators may be difficult to see in bright sunlight. What should you do?

▪ Put your indicator on earlier

▪ Give an arm signal as well as using your indicator

▪ Touch the brake several times to show the stop lights

▪ Turn as quickly as you can

Answer

▪ **Give an arm signal as well as using your indicator**

You should always ensure that other road users are aware of your intentions. If you feel your indicator might not be seen, give an arm signal as well.

Question 4.26

Mark two answers

You are riding at night. To be seen more easily you should

▪ ride with your headlight on dipped beam

▪ wear reflective clothing

▪ keep the motorcycle clean

▪ stay well out to the right

▪ wear waterproof clothing

Answers

▪ **ride with your headlight on dipped beam**

▪ **wear reflective clothing**

Reflective clothing works by reflecting light from the headlights of the other vehicles. This will make it easier for you to be seen. Fluorescent clothing, although effective during the day, won't show up as well as reflective clothing at night.

Mark two answers
When riding at night you should

- ride with your headlight on dipped beam
- wear reflective clothing
- wear a tinted visor
- ride in the centre of the road
- give arm signals

Answers

- **ride with your headlight on dipped beam**
- **wear reflective clothing**

Fluorescent clothing shows up in daylight, but at night you should wear reflective clothing. This could be a tabard or reflective body strap.

Mark three answers
You MUST use your headlight

- when riding in a group
- at night when street lighting is poor
- when carrying a passenger
- on motorways during darkness
- at times of poor visibility
- when parked on an unlit road

Answers

- **at night when street lighting is poor**
- **on motorways during darkness**
- **at times of poor visibility**

Your headlight is to help you see in the dark and to help other road users to see you. You must use your headlight at all times when visibility is seriously reduced, or at night

- on all roads where street lighting is more than 183 metres (600 feet) apart
- on all lit motorways.

Question 4.29

Mark one answer

When approaching a right-hand bend you should keep well to the left. Why is this?

- [ ] To improve your view of the road
- [ ] To overcome the effect of the road's slope
- [ ] To let faster traffic from behind overtake
- [ ] To be positioned safely if the motorcycle skids

Answer

- **To improve your view of the road**

Don't

- move over to the right to try and straighten the bend. You could endanger yourself by getting too close to oncoming traffic
- cross or straddle unbroken white lines along the centre of the road
- ride so fast that you can't stop within your range of vision.

Question 4.30

Mark three answers

You should not overtake when

- [ ] intending to turn left shortly afterwards
- [ ] in a one-way street
- [ ] approaching a junction
- [ ] riding up a long hill
- [ ] the view ahead is blocked

Answers

- **intending to turn left shortly afterwards**
- **approaching a junction**
- **the view ahead is blocked**

Before you overtake you should ask yourself if it's really necessary. Getting there safely is more important than taking unnecessary risks.

Question 4.31

Mark two answers

You are riding through a flood. Which TWO should you do?

- [ ] Keep in a high gear and stand up on the footrests
- [ ] Keep the engine running fast to keep water out of the exhaust
- [ ] Ride slowly and test your brakes when you are out of the water
- [ ] Turn your headlight off to avoid any electrical damage

Answers

- **Keep the engine running fast to keep water out of the exhaust**
- **Ride slowly and test your brakes when you are out of the water**

Take extra care when riding through flood water or fords. Ride through with high engine revs whilst partly slipping the clutch, to prevent water entering the exhaust system.

Try your brakes as soon as you are clear.

DSA THEORY TEST for motorcyclists

Question 4.32

Mark one answer

You have just ridden through a flood. When clear of the water you should test your

- starter motor
- headlight
- steering
- brakes

Answer

- brakes

If you have ridden through deep water your brakes may be less effective. Ride slowly whilst gently applying both brakes until normal braking is restored.

Question 4.33

Mark one answer

When going through flood water you should ride

- quickly in a high gear
- slowly in a high gear
- quickly in a low gear
- slowly in a low gear

Answer

- slowly in a low gear

If you have to go through a flood ride slowly in a low gear. Keep the engine running fast enough to keep water out of the exhaust. You may need to slip the clutch to do this.

Question 4.34

Mark two answers

You have to ride in foggy weather. You should

- stay close to the centre of the road
- switch only your sidelights on
- switch on your dipped headlights
- be aware of others not using their headlights
- always ride in the gutter to see the kerb

Answers

- switch on your dipped headlights
- be aware of others not using their headlights

Only travel in fog if your journey is absolutely necessary. Fog is often patchy and visibility can suddenly reduce without warning.

Question 4.35

Mark one answer

When riding at night you should NOT

- [ ] switch on full beam headlights
- [ ] overtake slower vehicles in front
- [ ] use dipped beam headlights
- [ ] use tinted glasses, lenses or visors

Answer

- [ ] **use tinted glasses, lenses or visors**

Do not use tinted glasses, lenses or visors at night because they reduce the amount of available light reaching your eyes. It's very important to keep your visor or goggles clean to give a clear view of the road at all times.

Question 4.36

Mark one answer

At a mini roundabout it is important that a motorcyclist should avoid

- [ ] turning right
- [ ] using signals
- [ ] taking lifesavers
- [ ] the painted area

Answer

- [ ] **the painted area**

Avoid riding over the painted area because these areas become very slippery especially when wet. Even on dry roads only a small part of the motorcycle's tyre makes contact with the road. Any reduction of grip can, therefore, affect the stability of your machine.

Question 4.37

Mark two answers

Which of the following should you do when riding in fog?

- [ ] Keep close to the vehicle in front
- [ ] Use your dipped headlight
- [ ] Ride close to the centre of the road
- [ ] Keep your visor or goggles clear
- [ ] Keep the vehicle in front in view

Answers

- [ ] **Use your dipped headlight**
- [ ] **Keep your visor or goggles clear**

Riding in fog presents extra risks. Make yourself visible and keep a sharp lookout for other road users.

Question 4.38

Mark two answers

You are riding on a motorway in a crosswind. You should take extra care when

- approaching service areas
- overtaking a large vehicle
- riding in slow moving traffic
- approaching an exit
- riding in exposed places

Question 4.39

Mark one answer

You have just gone through deep water. To dry off the brakes you should

- accelerate and keep to a high speed for a short time
- drive or ride slowly while pressing the brake pedal
- avoid using the brakes at all for a few miles
- stop for at least an hour to allow them time to dry

Answers

- **overtaking a large vehicle**
- **riding in exposed places**

Take extra care when overtaking large vehicles or riding on exposed places on windy days. Strong crosswinds can suddenly blow you off course. They can also affect the stability of other road others.

Answer

- **drive or ride slowly while pressing the brake pedal**

Water on the brake linings acts as a lubricant, causing the brakes to work less efficiently. Using the brakes lightly as you go along will dry the brakes out.

This section looks at judgement and hazard perception.

The questions will ask you about

- **Anticipation**

  plan ahead to prevent last-second reactions.

- **Hazard awareness**

  recognise a hazard ahead and prepare yourself for it.

- **Attention**

  look out for problems ahead when you're riding.

- **Speed and distance**

  be aware of the correct speed for the situation,
  leaving enough space to react.

- **Reaction time**

  be aware that you need time to react.

- **The effects of alcohol and drugs**

  understand how these will affect your reaction time.

- **Tiredness**

  don't ride if you're tired. You need to be alert at
  all times.

Question 5.1

Mark one answer

You see this sign on the rear of a slow-moving lorry that you want to pass. It is travelling in the middle lane of a three lane motorway. You should

- [ ] cautiously approach the lorry then pass on either side
- [ ] follow the lorry until you can leave the motorway
- [ ] wait on the hard shoulder until the lorry has stopped
- [ ] approach with care and keep to the left of the lorry

Answer

- ■ **approach with care and keep to the left of the lorry**

This sign indicates that you should keep to the left of the vehicle. If you wish to overtake, then you should do so on the left. Be aware that there might be workmen in the area.

Question 5.2

Mark two answers

Where would you expect to see these markers?

- [ ] On a motorway sign
- [ ] At the entrance to a narrow bridge
- [ ] On a large goods vehicle
- [ ] On a builder's skip placed on the road

Answers

- ■ **On a large goods vehicle**
- ■ **On a builder's skip placed on the road**

These markers are reflective so that they show up at night. If you see them ahead then you should be aware that there might be a stationary, slow or long vehicle.

Mark one answer

What does this signal from a police officer, mean to oncoming traffic?

▦ Go ahead

▦ Stop

▦ Turn left

▦ Turn right

Answer

▦ **Stop**

Police officers might be found at a point where there's heavy traffic or a breakdown of traffic lights. Check your copy of *The Highway Code* for the signals that they use.

Mark one answer

What is the main hazard shown in this picture?

▦ Vehicles turning right

▦ Vehicles doing U-turns

▦ The cyclist crossing the road

▦ Parked cars around the corner

Answer

▦ **The cyclist crossing the road**

Look at the picture carefully and try to imagine you're there. The cyclist in this picture isn't crossing the road in the correct place. You must be able to deal with the unexpected, especially when you're planning your approach to a hazardous junction. There will be several things to think about on your approach, so look well ahead to give yourself time to deal with them.

Question 5.5

Mark one answer

Which road user has caused a hazard?

▢ The parked car (arrowed A)

▢ The pedestrian waiting to cross (arrowed B)

▢ The moving car (arrowed C)

▢ The car turning (arrowed D)

Answer

▢ **The parked car (arrowed A)**

The car has parked on the approach to a pedestrian crossing. The road is marked with white zigzag lines. Don't park on these – they're there for a reason. Parking here will

• block the view for pedestrians wishing to cross the road

• restrict the view of the crossing for traffic approaching.

Question 5.6

Mark one answer

What should the driver of the car approaching the crossing do?

▢ Continue at the same speed

▢ Sound the horn

▢ Drive through quickly

▢ Slow down and get ready to stop

Answer

▢ **Slow down and get ready to stop**

Look well ahead to see if any hazards are developing. This will give you more time to deal with them in the correct way. The man in the picture is clearly intending to cross the road. You should be travelling at a speed that allows you to check your mirror, slow down and stop in good time. You shouldn't have to brake harshly.

Question 5.7

Mark one answer

What should the driver of the red car do?

- ◻ Wave the pedestrians who are waiting to cross
- ◻ Wait for the pedestrian in the road to cross
- ◻ Quickly drive behind the pedestrian in the road
- ◻ Tell the pedestrian in the road she should not have crossed

Answer

◻ **Wait for the pedestrian in the road to cross**

Some people might take longer to cross the road. They may be elderly or have a disability. Be patient and don't hurry them by showing your impatience. They might have poor eyesight or not be able to hear traffic approaching.

Don't signal or wave the pedestrian to cross the road. Other road users may not have seen your signal and this could lead the pedestrian into a hazardous situation.

Question 5.8

Mark three answers

What THREE things should the driver of the grey car (arrowed) be especially aware of?

- ◻ Pedestrians stepping out between cars
- ◻ Other cars behind the grey car
- ◻ Doors opening on parked cars
- ◻ The bumpy road surface
- ◻ Cars leaving parking spaces
- ◻ Empty parking spaces

Answers

◻ **Pedestrians stepping out between cars**

◻ **Doors opening on parked cars**

◻ **Cars leaving parking spaces**

Your awareness in hazardous situations is very important. In a busy street like the one in the picture there are many potential dangers. You might not be able to see a pedestrian crossing from between the parked vehicles. A driver or passenger of a parked car might open a door.

Ride at a speed that will allow you to stop in good time if a hazard suddenly appears. It could happen at any time.

Mark one answer

What should the driver of the red car (arrowed) do?

Sound the horn to tell other drivers where he is

Squeeze through the gap

Wave the driver of the white car to go on

Wait until the car blocking the way has moved

Answer

■ **Wait until the car blocking the way has moved**

If you're moving in slow-moving traffic think ahead so that you don't block junctions or stop others' progress. Don't

- force others to give way to you
- sound the horn to gain priority
- flash your lights to gain or give priority
- give any other misleading signal.

Question 5.10

Mark one answer

The red lights are flashing. What should you do when coming up to this level crossing?

Go through quickly

Go through carefully

Stop before the barrier

Switch on hazard warning lights

Answer

■ **Stop before the barrier**

Approach and cross level crossings with care. If you need to stop, wait patiently. In this picture there's a junction on the left, before the crossing; keep clear of the defined road markings. Don't

- try to beat the barrier by riding through
- ride onto the crossing unless the road is clear on the other side
- ride nose-to-tail over it
- stop on or just over the crossing.

Mark two answers

What are TWO main hazards you should be aware of when going along this street?

- ▨ Glare from the sun
- ▨ Car doors opening suddenly
- ▨ Lack of road markings
- ▨ The headlights on parked cars being switched on
- ▨ Large goods vehicles
- ▨ Children running out from between vehicles

Answers

- ▨ **Car doors opening suddenly**
- ▨ **Children running out from between vehicles**

When riding on roads where there are many parked vehicles you must take extra care. Always be ready for the unexpected and ride accordingly.

Children are small and you might not be able to see them about to emerge from between cars. Drivers may be getting in and out of their vehicles, providing another potential hazard. If the road is narrow, as it is in this picture, you'll also need to look well down the road. This will help you to deal with any oncoming traffic safely.

Mark one answer

What is the main hazard you should be aware of when following this cyclist?

- ▨ The cyclist may move into the left and dismount
- ▨ The cyclist may swerve out into the road
- ▨ The contents of the cyclist's carrier may fall onto the road
- ▨ The cyclist may wish to turn right at the end of the road

Answer

- ▨ **The cyclist may swerve out into the road**

When following a cyclist be aware that they also have to deal with the hazards around them. They may wobble or swerve to avoid a pot-hole in the road. They might see a potential hazard and change direction suddenly.

Don't ride very close to them or rev your engine impatiently. This will only add to their perception of a hazard and may rush them into a dangerous decision.

Question 5.13

Mark one answer

The driver of which car has caused a hazard?

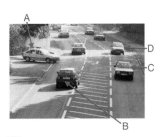

▣ Car A

▣ Car B

▣ Car C

▣ Car D

Answer

▣ **Car A**

The driver of car A has forced the approaching vehicle to the right onto the hatch-marked area of the road. It's also blocked the view of the other vehicle trying to emerge.

When dealing with busy junctions consider the other road users around you. Your actions must not put any other driver or rider at risk.

Question 5.14

Mark one answer

You think the driver of the vehicle in front has forgotten to cancel the right indicator. You should

▣ flash your lights to alert the driver

▣ sound your horn before overtaking

▣ overtake on the left if there is room

▣ stay behind and not overtake

Answer

▣ **stay behind and not overtake**

The driver may be unsure of the location of a junction and suddenly turn. Be cautious.

Mark one answer

What is the main hazard the driver of the red car (arrowed) should be most aware of?

■ Glare from the sun may affect the driver's vision

■ The black car may stop suddenly

■ The bus may move out into the road

■ Oncoming vehicles will assume the driver is turning right

Answer

■ **The bus may move out into the road**

You should try to anticipate the actions of the other road users around you. The driver of the red car should have made a mental note that the bus was at the bus stop. If you do this you'll be prepared for the bus pulling out. Look and see how many more passengers are waiting to board. If the last one has just got on, the bus is likely to move off.

Mark one answer

In heavy motorway traffic you are being followed closely by the vehicle behind. How can you lower the risk of an accident?

■ Increase your distance from the vehicle in front

■ Tap your foot on the brake pedal sharply

■ Switch on your hazard lights

■ Move onto the hard shoulder and stop

Answer

■ **Increase your distance from the vehicle in front**

On a busy motorway, traffic might still travel at high speeds although the weight of traffic means the vehicles are close together. Don't follow too close to the vehicle in front. If a driver behind seems to be 'pushing' you, increase your distance from the car in front by easing off the throttle. This will lessen the risk of an accident involving several vehicles.

DSA THEORY TEST for motorcyclists

Question 5.17

Mark one answer

You are travelling on this dual carriageway. Why may you need to slow down?

- There is a broken white line in the centre
- There are solid white lines either side
- There are roadworks ahead of you
- There are no footpaths

Answer

There are roadworks ahead of you

Look well ahead and read any road signs as you ride. They are there to inform you of what is ahead. In this case you may need to slow right down and change direction. Make sure you are well prepared for the hazard.

Question 5.18

Mark one answer

You see this sign ahead. You should expect the road to

- go steeply uphill
- go steeply downhill
- bend sharply to the left
- bend sharply to the right

Answer

bend sharply to the left

Adjust your speed in good time so that you are able to select the correct gear for the bend. Riding too fast into the bend will lead to lack of control.

Mark one answer

You are approaching this cyclist. You should

▓ overtake before the cyclist gets to the junction

▓ flash your headlights at the cyclist

▓ slow down and allow the cyclist to turn

▓ overtake the cyclist on the left-hand side

Answer

▓ **slow down and allow the cyclist to turn**

Keep well back and allow the cyclist room to take up the correct position for the turn. Don't ride up close behind or try to squeeze past through a narrow gap.

Question 5.20

Mark one answer

Why must you take extra care when turning right at this junction?

▓ Road surface is poor

▓ Footpaths are narrow

▓ Road markings are faint

▓ There is reduced visibility

Answer

▓ **There is reduced visibility**

You may have to pull forward slowly until you can see down the road. Be aware that the traffic approaching the junction can't see you either. If you don't know that it's clear, don't go

DSA THEORY TEST for motorcyclists

Question 5.21

Mark one answer

This yellow sign on a vehicle indicates this is

- a vehicle broken down
- a school bus
- an ice cream van
- a private ambulance

Answer

a school bus

Buses which carry children to and from school stop at places other than scheduled bus stops. Be aware that they might pull over to allow children to get on or off. This will normally be in rush hours when traffic is heavy.

Question 5.22

Mark one answer

When approaching this bridge you should give way to

- bicycles
- buses
- motorcycles
- cars

Answer

buses

A double-decker bus will have to take up a position in the centre of the road so that it can clear the bridge. There is normally a sign to indicate this. Look well down the road, through the bridge and consider that you may have to stop and give way to any bus approaching.

Mark one answer

What type of vehicle could you expect to meet in the middle of the road?

■ Lorry

■ Bicycle

■ Car

■ Motorcycle

Answer

■ **Lorry**

A large vehicle might have to take up all the road to allow the top of the vehicle to clear the bridge. The arch of the bridge is at its highest point in the centre.

Mark two answers

When approaching this hazard why should you slow down?

■ Because of the bend

■ Because its hard to see to the right

■ Because of approaching traffic

■ Because of animals crossing

■ Because of the level crossing

Answers

■ **Because of the bend**

■ **Because of the level crossing**

There are two hazards clearly signed in this picture. You should be preparing for the bend by slowing down and selecting the correct gear. You might also have to stop for the level crossing, so be alert and be prepared.

Question 5.25

Mark one answer

At this blind junction you must stop

- behind the line, then edge forward to see clearly
- beyond the line at a point where you can see clearly
- only if there is traffic on the main road
- only if you are turning to the right

Answer

■ **behind the line, then edge forward to see clearly**

The stop sign has been put here because it is a dangerous junction. You must stop. It will not be possible to assess the situation on the move, however slowly.

Question 5.26

Mark one answer

To ride you MUST be able to read a number plate from what distance?

- 10 metres (32 feet)
- 15 metres (50 feet)
- 20.5 metres (67 feet)
- 25.5 metres (84 feet)

Answer

■ **20.5 metres (67 feet)**

When you take your practical test your examiner will ask you to read a number plate from a distance of 20.5 metres (67 feet). This is a legal requirement to ensure that you can see situations around you on the road.

Question 5.27

Mark one answer

You are about to travel home. You cannot find the glasses you need to wear. You should

- go home slowly, keeping to quiet roads
- borrow a friend's glasses and use those
- go home at night, so that the lights will help you
- find a way of getting home without riding

Answer

- **find a way of getting home without riding**

Don't be tempted to ride if you've lost or forgotten your glasses. It's obvious that you must be able to see clearly when riding.

Question 5.28

Mark one answer

You find that you need glasses to read vehicle number plates at the required distance. When MUST you wear them?

- Only in bad weather conditions
- At all times when riding
- Only when you think it necessary
- Only in bad light or at night time

Answer

- **At all times when riding**

Have your eyesight tested before you start your practical training. Then, throughout your riding life, have periodical checks to ensure that your eyes haven't deteriorated.

Question 5.29

Mark three answers

Which THREE result from drinking alcohol?

- Less control
- A false sense of confidence
- Faster reactions
- Poor judgement of speed
- Greater awareness of danger

Answers

- **Less control**
- **A false sense of confidence**
- **Poor judgement of speed**

You must understand the dangers of mixing alcohol with riding. One drink is too many if you're going to ride. Alcohol will reduce your ability to ride safely.

Question 5.30

Mark three answers

Which THREE of these are likely effects of drinking alcohol?

- Reduced co-ordination
- Increased confidence
- Poor judgement
- Increased concentration
- Faster reactions
- Colour blindness

Answers

- **Reduced co-ordination**
- **Increased confidence**
- **Poor judgement**

Alcohol can increase confidence to a point where a rider's behaviour might become 'out of character'. Someone who normally behaves sensibly suddenly takes risks and enjoys it. Never let yourself or your friends get into this situation.

Question 5.31

Mark three answers

Drinking any amount of alcohol is likely to

- slow down your reactions to hazards
- increase the speed of your reactions
- worsen your judgement of speed
- improve your awareness of danger
- give a false sense of confidence

Answers

- **slow down your reactions to hazards**
- **worsen your judgement of speed**
- **give a false sense of confidence**

Never drink if you are going to ride. It's always the safest option not to drink at all. Don't be tempted, it's not worth it

Question 5.32

Mark three answers

What else can seriously affect your concentration, other than alcoholic drinks?

- Drugs
- Tiredness
- Tinted windows
- Contact lenses
- Loud music

Answers

- **Drugs**
- **Tiredness**
- **Loud music**

The least distraction can allow your concentration to drift. Think about your riding, and that only, to stay in full control of your motorcycle.

Mark one answer

Your doctor has given you a course of medicine. Why should you ask how it will affect you?

◼ Drugs make you a better driver or rider by quickening your reactions

◼ You will have to let your insurance company know about the medicine

◼ Some types of medicine can cause your reactions to slow down

◼ The medicine you take may affect your hearing

Answer

◼ **Some types of medicine can cause your reactions to slow down**

Always check the label of any medication container. The contents might affect your riding. If you aren't sure, ask your doctor or pharmacist.

Question 5.34

Mark two answers

You are not sure if your cough medicine will affect you. What TWO things could you do?

◼ Ask your doctor

◼ Check the medicine label

◼ ride if you feel alright

◼ Ask a friend or relative for advice

Answers

◼ **Ask your doctor**

◼ **Check the medicine label**

If you're taking medicine or drugs prescribed by your doctor, check to ensure that they won't make you drowsy. If you forget to ask at the time of your visit to the surgery, check with your pharmacist.

Question 5.35

Mark one answer

You are on a motorway. You feel tired. You should

◼ carry on but go slowly

◼ leave the motorway at the next exit

◼ complete your journey as quickly as possible

◼ stop on the hard shoulder

Answer

◼ **leave the motorway at the next exit**

If you do feel tired and there's no service station for many miles, leave the motorway at the next exit. Find a road off the motorway where you can pull up and stop safely.

Question 5.36

Mark one answer

You are planning a long journey. Do you need to plan rest stops?

- Yes, you should plan to stop every half an hour
- Yes, regular stops help concentration
- No, you will be less tired if you get there as soon as possible
- No, only fuel stops will be needed

Answer

Yes, regular stops help concentration

Try to plan your journey so that you can take rest stops. You may need to stop for something to eat in order to keep up your energy level. If this is allowed to drop you will become tired and lose concentration.

Question 5.37

Mark two answers

You get cold and wet when riding. Which TWO are likely to happen?

- You may lose concentration
- You may slide off the seat
- Your visor may freeze up
- Your reaction times may be slower
- Your helmet may loosen

Answers

You may lose concentration

Your reaction times may be slower

If you're riding a motorcycle you should ensure that you're wearing suitable clothing. If you become cold and uncomfortable this could cause you to lose concentration.

Question 5.38

Mark one answer

A driver pulls out of a side road in front of you. You have to brake hard. You should

- ignore the error and stay calm
- flash your lights to show your annoyance
- sound your horn to show your annoyance
- overtake as soon as possible

Answer

ignore the error and stay calm

If you're riding where there are a number of side roads, be alert. Drivers approaching or emerging from the side road might not be able to see you. Be especially careful if there are a lot of parked vehicles.

If a vehicle does emerge and you have to stop quickly

- try to be tolerant
- learn from the experience.

Question 5.39

Mark one answer

A driver does something that upsets you. You should

- [ ] try not to react
- [ ] let them know how you feel
- [ ] flash your headlights several times
- [ ] sound your horn

Answer

- [x] **try not to react**

There are occasions when other drivers or riders make a misjudgement or a mistake. If this happens try not to let it worry you. Don't react by showing anger. Sounding the horn, flashing the headlamps or shouting at the other driver won't help the situation. Good anticipation will help to prevent these incidents becoming accidents.

Question 5.40

Mark one answer

A driver's behaviour has upset you. It may help if you

- [ ] stop and take a break
- [ ] shout abusive language
- [ ] gesture to them with your hand
- [ ] follow their car, flashing the headlights

Answer

- [x] **stop and take a break**

Tiredness may make you more irritable than you would be normally. You might react differently to situations because of it. If you feel yourself becoming tense, take a break.

Question 5.41

Mark one answer

An elderly person's driving ability could be affected because they may be unable to

- [ ] obtain car insurance
- [ ] understand road signs
- [ ] react very quickly
- [ ] give signals correctly

Answer

- [x] **react very quickly**

Poor eyesight and hearing could affect their judgement of speed and distances. This may cause them to be more hesitant. Be tolerant of other drivers on the road and allow them time and room.

Question 5.42

Mark one answer

Why should you check over your shoulder before turning right into a side road?

- To make sure the road is clear
- To check for emerging traffic
- To check for overtaking vehicles
- To confirm your intention to turn

Answer

To check for overtaking vehicles

Take a last check over your shoulder before committing yourself to a manoeuvre. This is especially important when turning right.

Question 5.43

Mark one answer

What could happen if you do not keep to the left on right hand bends?

- You may not be able to see overtaking vehicles
- You may not be able to judge the sharpness of the bend
- Your head may cross over the centre line
- You may not be able to see vehicles to the rear

Answer

Your head may cross over the centre line

Do not ride too close to the centre line on right hand bends. It might mean that as you lean into the bend you put yourself in danger from oncoming vehicles.

Question 5.44

Mark one answer

You are riding up to a zebra crossing. You intend to stop for waiting pedestrians. How could you let them know you are stopping?

- By signalling with your left arm
- By waving them across
- By flashing your headlight
- By signalling with your right arm

Answer

By signalling with your right arm

Giving an arm signal would also indicate to any approaching vehicles as well as the pedestrians that you are stopping at the pedestrian crossing.

Mark one answer

You have just passed these warning lights. What hazard would you expect to see next?

⬛ A level crossing with no barrier

⬛ An ambulance station

⬛ A school crossing patrol

⬛ An opening bridge

Answer

⬛ **A school crossing patrol**

These lights warn of children crossing the road to a nearby school. Great care must be taken when the lights are operating.

Question 5.46

Mark one answer

Which of the following types of glasses should not be worn when riding at night?

⬛ Half-moon

⬛ Round

⬛ Bi-focal

⬛ Tinted

Answer

⬛ **Tinted**

If you are riding at night or in poor visibility, tinted lenses will reduce the efficiency of your vision, by reducing the amount of available light reaching your eyes.

Question 5.47

Mark two answers

Why should you be especially cautious when going past this bus?

There is traffic approaching in the distance

The driver may open the door

It may suddenly move off

People may cross the road in front of it

There are bicycles parked on the pavement

Answers

It may suddenly move off

People may cross the road in front of it

A stationary bus at a bus stop can hide pedestrians just in front of it who might be about to cross the road. Only ride past at a speed that will enable you to stop safely if you need to.

SECTION 6 · VULNERABLE ROAD USERS

This section looks at the risks when dealing with vulnerable road users.

The questions will ask you about

- **Pedestrians**

  be aware of their actions as they cross the road.

- **Children**

  be aware that they are particularly unpredictable on and around roads.

- **Elderly drivers**

  be aware that they may be slower to make decisions.

- **Disabled people**

  be aware that they might not be able to react to danger as quickly or easily as the able-bodied.

- **Cyclists**

  be aware that they may swerve to avoid obstructions and are often affected by weather conditions.

- **Motorcyclists**

  be aware of the presence of other motorcycles, scooters and mopeds.

- **Animals**

  be aware that animals can be unpredictable and may move slowly.

- **New drivers**

  be aware that they may be more hesitant, allow for this and be patient. They lack experience and are, therefore, more vulnerable.

Question 6.1

Mark one answer

You should not ride too closely behind a lorry because

- you will breathe in the lorry's exhaust fumes
- wind from the lorry will slow you down
- drivers behind you may not be able to see you
- it will reduce your view ahead

Answer

it will reduce your view ahead

If you're following a large vehicle your view beyond it will be restricted. Drop back. This will help you to see more of the road ahead.

Question 6.2

Mark one answer

You are riding in fast-flowing traffic. The vehicle behind is following too closely. You should

- slow down gradually to increase the gap in front of you
- slow down as quickly as possible by braking
- accelerate to get away from the vehicle behind you
- apply the brakes sharply to warn the driver behind

Answer

slow down gradually to increase the gap in front of you

Vehicles travelling too close together are dangerous. Increase the safety margin by dropping back.

Mark one answer

You are riding along a main road with many side roads. Why should you be particularly careful?

- Gusts of wind from the side roads may push you off course
- Drivers coming out from side roads may not see you
- The road will be more slippery where cars have been turning
- Drivers will be travelling slowly when they approach a junction

Answer

■ **Drivers coming out from side roads may not see you**

If you're riding along a main road where there are many side roads be alert. Drivers approaching or emerging from side roads may not be able to see you. Be especially careful if there are a lot of parked vehicles.

Always ride at a speed that will enable you to slow down and stop in good time. If you look well ahead and anticipate the actions of other road users you'll avoid having to brake suddenly or harshly.

Question 6.4

Mark one answer

You are on a country road. What should you expect to see coming towards you on YOUR side of the road?

- Motorcycles
- Bicycles
- Pedestrians
- Horse riders

Answer

■ **Pedestrians**

On a quiet country road always be aware that there may be a hazard just around the next bend, such as a slow-moving vehicle or pedestrians. There might not be a pavement and people may be walking on your side of the road.

Question 6.5

Mark one answer

Which sign means that there may be people walking along the road?

■   ■

■   ■

Answer

■

Always check the road signs as you ride. They'll keep you informed of hazards ahead and help you to anticipate any problems.

There are different types of signs showing pedestrians. Learn the meaning of each one. This will help you to be aware of the hazard ahead.

Question 6.6

Mark one answer

You are turning left into a side road. Pedestrians are crossing the road near the junction. You must

- wave them on
- sound your horn
- switch on your hazard lights
- wait for them to cross

Answer

- **wait for them to cross**

Before you turn into a junction check that it's clear. Check the pavement in each direction. If there are pedestrians crossing, let them cross in their own time.

Question 6.7

Mark one answer

You are turning left at a junction. Pedestrians have started to cross the road. You should

- go on, giving them plenty of room
- stop and wave at them to cross
- blow your horn and proceed
- give way to them

Answer

- **give way to them**

If you're turning into a side road you should give way to pedestrians already crossing. They have priority. Don't

- wave them across the road
- sound your horn
- flash your lights
- give any other misleading signal – other road users may misinterpret your signal and you might lead the pedestrian into a dangerous situation.

If a pedestrian is slow or indecisive, be patient and wait. Don't hurry them across by revving the engine.

Mark one answer

You are turning left from a main road into a side road. People are already crossing the road into which you are turning. You should

▓ continue, as it is your right of way

▓ signal to them to continue crossing

▓ wait and allow them to cross

▓ sound your horn to warn them of your presence

Answer

▓ **wait and allow them to cross**

Always check the road you're turning into. Approaching at the correct speed will allow you enough time to observe and react.

Mark one answer

You are at a road junction, turning into a minor road. There are pedestrians crossing the minor road. You should

▓ stop and wave the pedestrians across

▓ sound your horn to let the pedestrians know that you are there

▓ give way to the pedestrians who are already crossing

▓ carry on; the pedestrians should give way to you

Answer

▓ **give way to the pedestrians who are already crossing**

Always look into the road you're turning into. If there are pedestrians crossing, be considerate, but don't wave or signal to them to cross. Signal your intention to turn as you approach.

Question 6.10

Mark one answer

You are turning left into a side road. What hazards should you be especially aware of?

- One way street
- Pedestrians
- Traffic Congestion
- Parked vehicles

Answer

Pedestrians

Make sure that you have reduced you speed and are in the correct gear for the turn. Look into the road before you turn and always give way to any pedestrians who are crossing.

Question 6.11

Mark one answer

You intend to turn right into a side road. Just before turning you should check for motorcyclists who might be

- overtaking on your left
- following you closely
- emerging from the side road
- overtaking on your right

Answer

overtaking on your right

Never attempt to change direction to the right without checking your right-hand mirror. A motorcyclist might not have seen your signal, it could be hidden by the car behind you. This action should become a matter of routine.

Question 6.12

Mark one answer

As you approach a pelican crossing the lights change to green. Elderly people are halfway across. You should

- wave them to cross as quickly as they can
- rev your engine to make them hurry
- flash your lights in case they have not heard you
- wait because they will take longer to cross

Answer

wait because they will take longer to cross

Even if the lights turn to green, wait for them to clear the crossing. Allow them to cross the road in their own time.

Question 6.13

Mark one answer

A toucan crossing is different from other crossings because

- moped riders can use it
- it is controlled by a traffic warden
- it is controlled by two flashing lights
- cyclists can use it

Answer

cyclists can use it

Pedestrians and cyclists are shown the green light together. The signals are push button operated and there is no flashing amber phase.

Question 6.14

Mark two answers

At toucan crossings

- there is no flashing amber light
- cyclists are not permitted
- there is a continuously flashing amber beacon
- pedestrians and cyclists may cross
- you only stop if someone is waiting to cross

Answers

there is no flashing amber light

pedestrians and cyclists may cross

There are some crossings where cycle routes lead the cyclists to cross at the same place as pedestrians. Always look out for cyclists, as they're likely to be approaching faster than pedestrians.

Question 6.15

Mark one answer

What does this sign tell you?

- No cycling
- Cycle route ahead
- Route for cycles only
- End of cycle route

Answer

Cycle route ahead

With people's concern today for the environment, cycle routes are being created in our towns and cities. These can be defined by road markings and signs. Don't ride in them. Respect the presence of cyclists on the road and give them plenty of room if you need to pass.

Question 6.16

Mark one answer

How will a school crossing patrol signal you to stop?

- By pointing to children on the opposite pavement
- By displaying a red light
- By displaying a stop sign
- By giving you an arm signal

Answer

■ **By displaying a stop sign**

If someone steps out into the road with a school crossing sign you must stop. Don't

- wave anyone across the road
- get impatient or rev your engine.

Question 6.17

Mark one answer

Where would you see this sign?

- In the window of a car taking children to school
- At the side of the road
- At playground areas
- On the rear of a school bus or coach

Answer

■ **On the rear of a school bus or coach**

Vehicles that are used to carry children to and from school will be travelling at busy times of the day. If you're following a vehicle with this sign, be prepared for it to make frequent stops. It might pick up or set down passengers in places other than normal bus stops.

Question 6.18

Mark one answer

Where would you see this sign?

- Near a school crossing
- At a playground entrance
- On a school bus
- At a 'pedestrians only' area

Answer

- **On a school bus**

Watch out for children crossing the road from the other side of the bus.

Question 6.19

Mark one answer

You are parking your motorcycle in the street. The car parked in front of you is displaying an orange badge. You should

- park close to it to save road space
- allow room for a wheelchair
- wait until the orange-badge holder returns
- park with two wheels on the pavement

Answer

- **allow room for a wheelchair**

Think about the room that's needed to open the rear of the vehicle and lift a wheelchair in. Room might be needed to manoeuvre a wheelchair between the vehicle and your motorcycle.

Question 6.20

Mark one answer

You are following a car driven by an elderly driver. You should

- expect the driver to drive badly
- flash your lights and overtake
- be aware that the driver's reactions may not be as fast as yours
- stay very close behind but be careful

Answer

- **be aware that the driver's reactions may not be as fast as yours**

You must show consideration to other road users. Their reactions may be slower and they might need more time to deal with a situation. Be tolerant and don't lose patience or show your annoyance.

Question 6.21

Mark one answer

Which sign tells you that pedestrians may be walking in the road as there is no pavement?

Answer

If you have to pass pedestrians who are walking at the side of the road, you must give them plenty of room. The draught caused by your motorcycle could unsteady them, or they could turn around when they hear your engine and step sideways into the road.

Question 6.22

Mark one answer

What does this sign mean?

☐ No route for pedestrians and cyclists

☐ A route for pedestrians only

☐ A route for cyclists only

☐ A route for pedestrians and cyclists

Answer

■ **A route for pedestrians and cyclists**

This shared route is for pedestrians and cyclists only. Be aware that when it ends the cyclists will be rejoining the main road.

Question 6.23

Mark one answer

You see a pedestrian with a white stick and red band. This means that the person is

☐ physically disabled

☐ deaf only

☐ blind only

■ deaf and blind

Answer

■ **deaf and blind**

If the person is deaf as well as blind the stick will have a red reflective band. You can't tell if a pedestrian is deaf. Don't assume everyone can hear you approaching.

Question 6.24

Mark one answer

You are riding towards a zebra crossing. Waiting to cross is a person in a wheelchair. You should

- continue on your way
- wave to the person to cross
- wave to the person to wait
- be prepared to stop

Answer

be prepared to stop

As you would with an able bodied pedestrian, you should prepare to slow down and stop. Don't wave the pedestrian across as, due to their seated position, they might not be able to see traffic beyond in a right hand lane.

Question 6.25

Mark one answer

What action would you take when elderly people are crossing the road?

- Wave them across so they know that you have seen them
- Be patient and allow them to cross in their own time
- Rev the engine to let them know that you are waiting
- Tap the horn in case they are hard of hearing

Answer

Be patient and allow them to cross in their own time

Don't hurry elderly people across the road by riding up close to them or revving the engine. Be aware that they might take longer to cross. They might also be hard of hearing and not able to hear your approach.

Question 6.26

Mark one answer

You see two elderly pedestrians about to cross the road ahead. You should

- expect them to wait for you to pass
- speed up to get past them quickly
- stop and wave them across the road
- be careful, they may misjudge your speed

Answer

be careful, they may misjudge your speed

Their concentration, judgement, hearing and/or vision could be impaired. Be aware that if they proceed to cross they will take more time to do so.

DSA THEORY TEST for motorcyclists

Question 6.27

Mark one answer

You are following a motorcyclist on an uneven road. You should

- allow less room so you can be seen in their mirrors
- overtake immediately
- allow extra room in case they swerve to avoid pot-holes
- allow the same room as normal because road surfaces do not affect motorcyclists

Answer

■ **allow extra room in case they swerve to avoid pot-holes**

Pot-holes in the road can unsteady a motorcyclist. For this reason the rider might swerve to avoid an uneven road surface. Watch out at places where this is likely to occur.

Question 6.28

Mark one answer

What does this sign mean?

- Contra-flow pedal cycle lane
- With-flow pedal cycle lane
- Pedal cycles and buses only
- No pedal cycles or buses

Answer

■ **With-flow pedal cycle lane**

This will be marked on the road, sometimes with a different colour surface. Leave these clear for cyclists and don't pass too closely when you overtake.

Question 6.29

Mark one answer

You should NEVER attempt to overtake a cyclist

- just before you turn left
- just before you turn right
- on a one-way street
- on a dual carriageway

Answer

■ **just before you turn left**

If you want to turn left and there's a cyclist in front of you, hold back. Wait until the cyclist has passed the junction and then turn left behind them.

Mark one answer

You are following a cyclist. You wish to turn left just ahead. You should

■ overtake the cyclist before the junction

■ pull alongside the cyclist and stay level until after the junction

■ hold back until the cyclist has passed the junction

■ go around the cyclist on the junction

Answer

■ **hold back until the cyclist has passed the junction**

When riding make allowances for cyclists. Allow them plenty of room. If you're following a cyclist, be aware that they also have to deal with hazards around them. The might swerve or change direction suddenly t avoid an uneven road surface.

Mark one answer

You are coming up to a roundabout. A cyclist is signalling to turn right. What should you do?

■ Overtake on the right

■ Give a horn warning

■ Signal the cyclist to move across

■ Give the cyclist plenty of room

Answer

■ **Give the cyclist plenty of room**

If you're following a cyclist who's signalling to turn right at a roundabout leave plenty of room. Give them space and time to get into the correct lane.

Mark one answer

You are following two cyclists. They approach a roundabout in the left-hand lane. In which direction should you expect the cyclists to go?

■ Left

■ Right

■ Any direction

■ Straight ahead

Answer

■ **Any direction**

If you're following a cyclist into a roundabout be aware of them as they might not be taking the exit you anticipate. Cyclists approaching in the left-hand lane may be turning right but may not have been able to get into the correct lane due to heavy traffic. Give them room.

DSA THEORY TEST for motorcyclists

Question 6.33

Mark one answer

You are approaching this roundabout and see the cyclist signal right. Why is the cyclist keeping to the left?

- It is a quicker route for the cyclist
- The cyclist is going to turn left instead
- The cyclist thinks *The Highway Code* does not apply to bicycles
- The cyclist is slower and more vulnerable

Question 6.34

Mark one answer

When you are overtaking a cyclist you should leave as much room as you would give to a car. What is the main reason for this?

- The cyclist might change lanes
- The cyclist might get off the bike
- The cyclist might swerve
- The cyclist might have to make a right turn

Answer

The cyclist is slower and more vulnerable

Cycling in today's heavy traffic can be hazardous. Some cyclists may not feel happy about crossing the path of traffic to take up a position in an outside lane. Be aware of this and understand that, although in the left-hand lane, the cyclist might be turning right.

Answer

The cyclist might swerve

If you intend to overtake a cyclist look at the road ahead. Check if the cyclist needs to change direction for a parked vehicle or an uneven road surface. When you have a safe place to overtake, leave as much room as you would for a car. Don't cut in sharply or pass too closely.

Mark two answers

Which TWO should you allow extra room when overtaking?

- Motorcycles
- Tractors
- Bicycles
- Road-sweeping vehicles

Answers

- **Motorcycles**
- **Bicycles**

Don't pass riders too closely as this may cause them to lose balance. Always leave as much room as you would for a car, and don't cut in.

Mark one answer

Why should you allow extra room when overtaking a motorcyclist on a windy day?

- The rider may turn off suddenly to get out of the wind
- The rider may be blown across in front of you
- The rider may stop suddenly
- The rider may be travelling faster than normal

Answer

- **The rider may be blown across in front of you**

A motorcyclist's position on the road can be affected by high winds. If you're riding on a windy day be aware that the conditions might force a motorcyclist to swerve or wobble. Take this into consideration if you're following or wish to overtake.

Mark one answer

Why should you look particularly for motorcyclists and cyclists at junctions?

- They may want to turn into the side road
- They may slow down to let you turn
- They are harder to see
- They might not see you turn

Answer

- **They are harder to see**

These road users could be hazards that are hidden from your view. Parked cars could cause you to lose sight of them. Consider that cyclists may need more time to make a turn.

Question 6.38

Mark one answer

You are waiting to come out of a side road. Why should you watch carefully for motorcycles?

■ Motorcycles are usually faster than cars

■ Police patrols often use motorcycles

■ Motorcycles are small and hard to see

■ Motorcycles have right of way

Answer

■ **Motorcycles are small and hard to see**

If you're waiting to emerge from a side road, watch out for motorcyclists. They're smaller and more difficult to see. Be especially careful if there are parked vehicles restricting your view. There might be a motorcyclist approaching.

IF YOU DON'T KNOW, DON'T GO.

Question 6.39

Mark one answer

Where should you take particular care to look out for motorcyclists and cyclists?

■ On dual carriageways

■ At junctions

■ At zebra crossings

■ On one-way streets

Answer

■ **At junctions**

Motorcyclists and cyclists may be more difficult to see on the road. This is especially the case at junctions. You may not be able to see a motorcyclist approaching a junction if your view's blocked by other traffic. Be aware of the possibility. A motorcycle may be travelling as fast as a car, or faster. Make sure that you judge speeds correctly before you emerge.

Question 6.40

Mark one answer

In daylight, an approaching motorcyclist is using a dipped headlight. Why?

■ So that the rider can be seen more easily

■ To stop the battery overcharging

■ To improve the rider's vision

■ The rider is inviting you to proceed

Answer

■ **So that the rider can be seen more easily**

A motorcycle can be lost out of sight behind another vehicle. The use of the headlight helps to make it more conspicuous and therefore more easily seen.

Mark one answer

Where in particular should you look out for other motorcyclists?

▨ In a filling station

▨ At a road junction

▨ Near a service area

▨ When entering a car park

Answer

▨ **At a road junction**

Always look ahead and try to make use of the information you see. This will enable you to anticipate possible hazards, and give you more time to deal with them as they occur.

Question 6.42

Mark one answer

Motorcyclists should wear bright clothing mainly because

▨ they must do so by law

▨ it helps keep them cool in summer

▨ the colours are popular

▨ drivers often do not see them

Answer

▨ **drivers often do not see them**

Although they're advised to wear clothing that's bright or reflective, motorcyclists often wear black. This means that they're difficult to see. Look out for them.

Question 6.43

Mark one answer

There is a slow-moving motorcyclist ahead of you. You are unsure what the rider is going to do. You should

▨ pass on the left

▨ pass on the right

▨ stay behind

▨ move closer

Answer

▨ **stay behind**

Be patient. The motorcyclist might be turning right or changing direction.

Question 6.44

Mark one answer

You are travelling behind a moped. You want to turn left just ahead. You should

- overtake the moped before the junction
- pull alongside the moped and stay level until just before the junction
- sound your horn as a warning and pull in front of the moped
- stay behind until the moped has passed the junction

Answer

- **stay behind until the moped has passed the junction**

Passing the moped and turning into the junction could mean that you cut across the front of the rider. This might force them to slow down, stop or even lose control.

Question 6.45

Mark one answer

Motorcyclists will often look round over their right shoulder just before turning right. This is because

- they need to listen for following traffic
- motorcycles do not have mirrors
- looking around helps them balance as they turn
- they need to check for traffic in their blind area

Answer

- **they need to check for traffic in their blind area**

If you're behind a motorcyclist who makes a quick glance over their shoulder expect them to be changing direction. They should do this before turning. By observing this you'll get an early signal of their intention.

Question 6.46

Mark three answers

At road junctions which of the following are most vulnerable?

- Cyclists
- Motorcyclists
- Pedestrians
- Car drivers
- Lorry drivers

Answers

- **Cyclists**
- **Motorcyclists**
- **Pedestrians**

Good effective observation, coupled with appropriate action, can save lives.

Question 6.47

Mark one answer

Motorcyclists are particularly vulnerable

- when moving off
- on dual carriageways
- when approaching junctions
- on motorways

Answer

- **when approaching junctions**

Another road user failing to see a motorcyclist at a junction is a major cause of collision accidents. Wherever streams of traffic join or cross there's the potential for this type of accident to occur. Ride defensively and make yourself easy to see by wearing bright clothing.

Question 6.48

Mark three answers

Which THREE of the following are hazards motorcyclists present in queues of traffic?

- Cutting in just in front of you
- Riding in single file
- Passing very close to you
- Riding with their headlight on dipped beam
- Filtering between the lanes

Answers

- **Cutting in just in front of you**
- **Passing very close to you**
- **Filtering between the lanes**

Where there's more than one lane of queuing traffic, motorcyclists use the opportunity to make progress by riding between the lanes. Be aware that they may be passing on either side. Check your mirrors before you move off.

Question 6.49

Mark one answer

Ahead of you there is a vehicle with a flashing amber beacon. This means it is

- slow moving
- broken down
- a doctor's car
- a school crossing patrol

Answer

- **slow moving**

As you approach the vehicle assess the situation. Due to it's slow progress you will need to judge whether it is safe to overtake.

Question 6.50

Mark one answer

An injured motorcyclist is lying unconscious in the road. You should

☐ remove the safety helmet

☐ seek medical assistance

☐ move the person off the road

☐ remove the leather jacket

Answer

☐ **seek medical assistance**

In an injury situation the earlier proper medical attention is given the better. Either send someone to phone for help or go yourself. Only move an injured person if further danger is threatened.

Do Not Remove The Safety Helmet.

Question 6.51

Mark three answers

You are riding on a country lane. You see cattle on the road. You should

☐ slow down

☐ stop if necessary

☐ give plenty of room

☐ rev your engine

☐ sound your horn

☐ ride up close behind them

Answers

☐ **slow down**

☐ **stop if necessary**

☐ **give plenty of room**

Try not to startle the animals. They can be easily frightened by noise or by traffic passing too closely.

Question 6.52

Mark two answers

You are about to overtake horse riders. Which TWO of the following could scare the horses?

☐ Sounding your horn

☐ Giving arm signals

☐ Riding slowly

☐ Revving your engine

Answer

☐ **Sounding your horn**

☐ **Revving your engine**

When passing horses allow plenty of space and slow down. Animals can become frightened by sudden or loud noises, so don't sound your horn or rev the engine.

Mark one answer

You notice horse riders in front. What should you do FIRST?

Pull out to the middle of the road

Be prepared to slow down

Accelerate around them

Signal right

Answer

Be prepared to slow down

When riding you must always look well ahead and be ready to deal with hazards as they occur.

Question 6.54

Mark one answer

You are on a narrow country road. Where would you find it most difficult to see horses and riders ahead of you?

On left-hand bends

When travelling downhill

When travelling uphill

On right-hand bends

Answer

On left-hand bends

You're more likely to come across horses on country roads. These roads can be narrow, so extra care must be taken when approaching left-hand bends as your view of the road ahead will be restricted.

Question 6.55

Mark one answer

A horse rider is in the left-hand lane approaching a roundabout. You should expect the rider to

go in any direction

turn right

turn left

go ahead

Answer

go in any direction

Horses and their riders will move more slowly than other road users. They might not have time to cut across busy traffic to take up positions in the offside lane. For this reason a horse and rider may approach a roundabout in the left-hand lane, even though they're turning right.

DSA THEORY TEST for motorcyclists

Question 6.56

Mark two answers

You are approaching a roundabout. There are horses just ahead of you. You should

- be prepared to stop
- treat them like any other vehicle
- give them plenty of room
- accelerate past as quickly as possible
- sound your horn as a warning

Answer

- **be prepared to stop**
- **give them plenty of room**

Horse riders often keep to the outside of the roundabout even if they are turning right. Give them room in case they have to cross lanes of traffic.

Question 6.57

Mark one answer

You see a horse rider as you approach a roundabout. They are signalling right but keeping well to the left. You should

- proceed as normal
- keep close to them
- cut in front of them
- stay well back

Answer

- **stay well back**

Allow the riders to enter and exit the roundabout in their own time. Don't ride up close behind or alongside them, as this could disturb the horses.

Mark three answers

Which THREE should you do when passing sheep on a road?

- [ ] Allow plenty of room
- [ ] Go very slowly
- [ ] Pass quickly but quietly
- [ ] Be ready to stop
- [ ] Briefly sound your horn

Answers

- ■ **Allow plenty of room**
- ■ **Go very slowly**
- ■ **Be ready to stop**

If you see animals in the road ahead slow down and be ready to stop. Animals are easily frightened by

- noise
- vehicles passing too close to them.

Stop if signalled to do so by the person in charge. Switch off your engine if the animals are taking a long time to clear the road.

Question 6.59

Mark one answer

Riders are more likely to have a serious accident if they

- [ ] wear glasses or contact lenses
- [ ] have recently passed their test
- [ ] are carrying pillion passengers
- [ ] have not taken a theory test

Answer

- ■ **have recently passed their test**

It takes time to experience different situations on the road. Develop safe habits and a responsible attitude from the start. This will help you to become a better rider.

Question 6.60

Mark one answer

How would you react to drivers who appear to be inexperienced?

- [ ] Sound your horn to warn them of your presence
- [ ] Be patient and prepare for them to react more slowly
- [ ] Flash your headlights to indicate that it is safe for them to proceed
- [ ] Overtake them as soon as possible

Answer

- ■ **Be patient and prepare for them to react more slowly**

Learners might not have confidence when they first start to drive. Allow them plenty of room and don't react adversely to their hesitation. We all learn from experience, but new drivers will have had less practice in dealing with all the situations that might occur.

Question 6.61

Mark one answer

You have just passed your test. How can you decrease your risk of accidents on the motorway?

- By keeping up with the car in front
- By never going over 40 mph
- By staying only in the left-hand lane
- By taking further training

Answer

By taking further training

You're more likely to have an accident in the first year after taking your test. Lack of experience means that you might not react to hazards as quickly as a more experienced rider. Further training will help you to become safer on the roads.

As a motorcyclist you should ask your Compulsory Basic Training (CBT) instructor about this.

Question 6.62

Mark one answer

Which age group is most likely to be involved in a road accident?

- 36 to 45-year-olds
- 55-year-olds and over
- 46 to 55-year-olds
- 17 to 25-year-olds

Answer

17 to 25-year-olds

Statistics show that if you're between the ages of 17 and 25 you're more likely to be involved in a road accident. There are several reasons contributing to this, but in most cases accidents are due to rider error.

Question 6.63

Mark one answer

You are following a learner driver who stalls at a junction. You should

- be patient as you expect them to make mistakes
- stay very close behind and flash your headlights
- start to rev your engine if they take too long to restart
- immediately steer around them and drive on

Answer

be patient as you expect them to make mistakes

Learning is a process of practice and experience. Try to understand this and tolerate others who are at the beginning of this process.

Question 6.64

Mark one answer

A learner driver has begun to emerge into your path from a side road on the left. You should

- be ready to slow down and stop
- let them emerge then ride close behind
- turn into the side road
- brake hard, then wave them out

Answer

be ready to slow down and stop

If you see another vehicle begin to emerge into your path you should ride defensively. Always be ready to slow down or stop if necessary.

Question 6.65

Mark one answer

The vehicle ahead is being driven by a learner. You should

- keep calm and be patient
- ride up close behind
- put your headlight on full beam
- sound your horn and overtake

Answer

keep calm and be patient

Learners might take longer to react to traffic situations. Don't unnerve them by riding up close behind.

Question 6.66

Mark one answer

At night you see a pedestrian wearing reflective clothing and carrying a bright red light. What does this mean?

- You are approaching roadworks
- You are approaching an organised walk
- You are approaching a slow-moving vehicle
- You are approaching an accident black spot

Answer

You are approaching an organised walk

The people involved in the march should be keeping to the left, but this can't be assumed. Pass slowly, ensuring that you have the time to do so safely. Be aware that the pedestrians have their backs to you and might not know that you're there.

DSA **THEORY TEST** for motorcyclists

Question 6.67

Mark one answer

There are flashing amber lights under a school warning sign. What action should you take?

- Reduce speed until you are clear of the area
- Keep up your speed and sound the horn
- Increase your speed to clear the area quickly
- Wait at the lights until they change to green

Answer

Reduce speed until you are clear of the area

The flashing amber lights are switched on to warn you that children may be crossing near a school.

Question 6.68

Mark one answer

Why is it vital for a rider to make a lifesaver check before turning right?

- To check for any overtaking traffic
- To confirm that they are about to turn
- To make sure the side road is clear
- To check that the rear indicator is flashing

Answer

To check for any overtaking traffic

The lifesaver glance is what it says. This action makes you aware of what is happening behind and alongside before you alter your course. This glance must be timed so that you still have time to react if it isn't safe to carry out your manoeuvre.

Question 6.69

Mark one answer

Which of the following types of crossing can detect when people are on them?

- Pelican
- Toucan
- Zebra
- Puffin

Answer

Puffin

'Puffin' is an acronym for **p**edestrian **u**ser **f**riendly **in**telligent crossing. Sensors detect when people are crossing and will hold the waiting traffic on a red signal until the pedestrians are clear.

Mark one answer

The road outside this school is marked with yellow zig zag lines. What do these lines mean?

Answer

■ **You must not wait or park your motorcycle here at all**

Parking here will block the view of the school gates. Doing this will endanger the lives of children on their way to and from school.

■ You may park on the lines when dropping off school children

■ You may park on the lines when picking school children up

■ You must not wait or park your motorcycle here at all

■ You must stay with your motorcycle if you park here

Question 6.71

Mark one answer

You are approaching this crossing. You should

Answer

■ prepare to slow down and stop

Be courteous and prepare to stop. Do not wave people across as this could be dangerous if another vehicle is approaching the crossing.

■ prepare to slow down and stop

■ stop and wave the pedestrians across

■ speed up and pass by quickly

■ drive on unless the pedestrians step out

Question 6.72

Mark one answer

You see a pedestrian with a dog. The dog has a bright orange lead and collar. This especially warns you that the pedestrian is

- [ ] elderly
- [ ] dog training
- [ ] colour blind
- [ ] deaf

Answer

- [ ] **deaf**

Take extra care as the pedestrian is more vulnerable. Always be aware that this pedestrian may not hear you.

This section looks at the risks when dealing with different types of vehicle.

The questions will ask you about

- **Motorcycles**

  be aware that other motorcycles, scooters and mopeds may need as much room as a car.

- **Lorries**

  are larger and need more room on the road.

- **Buses**

  are usually large and might make frequent stops.

Question 7.1

Mark one answer

The road is wet. Why might a motorcyclist steer round drain covers on a bend?

- To avoid puncturing the tyres on the edge of the drain covers
- To prevent the motorcycle sliding on the metal drain covers
- To help judge the bend using the drain covers as marker points
- To avoid splashing pedestrians on the pavement

Answer

■ **To prevent the motorcycle sliding on the metal drain covers**

The actions other drivers take may be due to the size or characteristics of their vehicle. If you understand this it will help you to anticipate their actions.

Motorcyclists will be checking the road ahead for uneven or slippery surfaces, especially in wet weather. They may need to move across their lane to avoid road surface hazards.

Question 7.2

Mark one answer

You are about to overtake a slow-moving motorcyclist. Which one of these signs would make you take special care?

Answer

In windy weather watch out for motorcyclists, as they can be blown sideways and veer into your path. Pass them leaving plenty of room and check your mirror as you pass and pull back in.

Question 7.3

Mark one answer

You are waiting to emerge left from a minor road. A large vehicle is approaching from the right. You have time to turn, but you should wait. Why?

- The large vehicle can easily hide an overtaking vehicle
- The large vehicle can turn suddenly
- The large vehicle is difficult to steer in a straight line
- The large vehicle can easily hide vehicles from the left

Answer

- **The large vehicle can easily hide an overtaking vehicle**

Don't only consider the hazards you can see. The hidden, possible hazards are the most dangerous as they are often unexpected. By considering the possible dangers when emerging, you can lessen the risk.

Question 7.4

Mark one answer

You are following a large articulated vehicle. It is going to turn left into a narrow road. What action should you take?

- Move out and overtake on the right
- Pass on the left as the vehicle moves out
- Be prepared to stop behind
- Overtake quickly before the lorry moves out

Answer

- **Be prepared to stop behind**

Lorries are larger and longer than other vehicles. This will affect their position when approaching junctions – especially when turning left. They need more room so that they don't cut in and mount the kerb when turning.

Question 7.5

Mark one answer

You are following a long vehicle. It approaches a crossroads and signals left, but moves out to the right. You should

- get closer in order to pass it quickly
- stay well back and give it room
- assume the signal is wrong and it is really turning right
- overtake as it starts to slow down

Question 7.6

Mark one answer

You are riding behind a long vehicle. There is a mini-roundabout ahead. The vehicle is signalling left, but positioned to the right. You should

- sound your horn
- overtake on the left
- keep well back
- flash your headlights

Answer

■ **stay well back and give it room**

Approaching a left turn a lorry may swing out to the right. This is to allow the rear wheels to clear the kerb as it turns. If you see a gap on the nearside don't try to filter through.

Answer

■ **keep well back**

The long vehicle needs more room to make the left turn. Don't overtake on the left. Staying well back will also give you a better view around the vehicle.

Mark one answer

You are following a long vehicle approaching a crossroads. The driver signals right but moves close to the left-hand kerb. What should you do?

- ▨ Warn the driver of the wrong signal
- ▨ Wait behind the long vehicle
- ▨ Report the driver to the police
- ▨ Overtake on the right-hand side

Answer

▨ **Wait behind the long vehicle**

When a long vehicle is going to turn right it may need to keep close to the left-hand kerb. This is to prevent the rear end of the trailer cutting the corner. You need to be aware of how long vehicles behave in such situations. Don't overtake the lorry because it could turn as you're alongside. Stay behind and give plenty of room.

Mark one answer

You are approaching a mini-roundabout. The long vehicle in front is signalling left but positioned over to the right. You should

- ▨ sound your horn
- ▨ overtake on the left
- ▨ follow the same course as the lorry
- ▨ keep well back

Answer

▨ **keep well back**

At mini-roundabouts there isn't much room for a long vehicle to manoeuvre. It will have to swing out wide so that it can complete the turn safely. Keep well back and allow plenty of room. Don't ride along its nearside.

DSA THEORY TEST for motorcyclists

Mark one answer

You are following a large vehicle. Side and end markers are being displayed. This means the load

- is higher than normal
- may be flammable
- is in two parts
- overhangs at the rear

Answer

■ **overhangs at the rear**

Always keep a safe distance from the vehicle in front. In this case you should judge your separation distance from the extreme rear of the load the vehicle is carrying.

Question 7.10

Mark one answer

You keep well back while waiting to overtake a large vehicle. A car fills the gap. You should

- sound your horn
- drop back further
- flash your headlights
- start to overtake

Answer

■ **drop back further**

It's very frustrating when your separation distance is shortened by another car. React positively and consider your own and your passengers safety.

Question 7.11

Mark one answer

Before overtaking a large vehicle you should keep well back. Why is this?

- To give acceleration space to overtake quickly on blind bends
- To get the best view of the road ahead
- To leave a gap in case the vehicle stops and rolls back
- To offer other drivers a safe gap if they want to overtake you

Answer

■ **To get the best view of the road ahead**

When following a large vehicle keep well back. If you're too close

- you won't be able to see the road ahead
- the driver of the long vehicle might not be able to see you in his mirrors.

Mark one answer

You wish to overtake a long, slow moving vehicle on a busy road. You should

☐ follow it closely and keep moving out to see the road ahead

☐ flash your headlights for the oncoming traffic to give way

☐ stay behind until the driver waves you past

☐ keep well back until you can see that it is clear

Answer

☐ **keep well back until you can see that it is clear**

If you wish to overtake a long vehicle, stay well back so that you can see the road ahead

Don't

- get up close to the vehicle – this will restrict your view of the road ahead
- get impatient – overtaking on a busy road calls for sound judgement
- take a gamble – only overtake when you can see that you can safely complete the manoeuvre
- flash your headlights – this could confuse and mislead other traffic
- sound your horn.

Mark one answer

Why is passing a lorry more risky than passing a car?

☐ Lorries are longer than cars

☐ Lorries may suddenly pull up

☐ The brakes of lorries are not as good

☐ Lorries climb hills more slowly

Answer

☐ **Lorries are longer than cars**

Hazards to watch for include

- oncoming traffic
- junctions
- bends or dips, which could restrict your view
- any signs or road markings prohibiting overtaking.

Never begin to overtake unless you can see that it's safe to complete the manoeuvre.

Question 7.14

Mark one answer

You are riding along a road and you see this signal. It means

- cars must stop
- trams must stop
- both trams and cars must stop
- both trams and cars can continue

Answer

trams must stop

Trams are popular in some cities, not least because they don't create fumes so they're cleaner. You may not live in an area that has trams, but you should still learn the signs. You never know when you might ride through a town that has them.

Question 7.15

Mark two answers

You are travelling behind a bus that pulls up at a bus stop. What should you do?

- Accelerate past the bus sounding your horn
- Watch carefully for pedestrians
- Be ready to give way to the bus
- Pull in closely behind the bus

Answers

Watch carefully for pedestrians

Be ready to give way to the bus

There might be pedestrians crossing from in front of the bus. Look out for them if you intend to pass. Consider staying back and waiting.

How many people are waiting to get on the bus? Check the queue if you can. The bus might be moving off straight away.

Question 7.16

Mark one answer

When you approach a bus signalling to move off from a bus stop you should

◻ get past before it moves

◻ allow it to pull away, if it is safe to do so

◻ flash your headllights as you approach

◻ signal left and wave the bus on

Question 7.17

Mark one answer

Which of these vehicles is LEAST likely to be affected by crosswinds?

◻ Cyclists

◻ Motorcyclists

◻ High-sided vehicles

◻ Cars

Answer

◻ **allow it to pull away, if it is safe to do so**

Give way to buses whenever you can do so safely, especially when they signal to pull away from bus stops. Look out for people who've got off the bus and may try to cross the road. Don't

• try to accelerate past before it moves away

• flash your lights – other road users may be misled by this signal.

Answer

◻ **Cars**

Crosswinds can take you by surprise

• after overtaking a large vehicle

• when passing gaps between hedges or buildings

• on exposed sections of road.

DSA THEORY TEST for motorcyclists

Question 7.18

Mark one answer

You are following a large lorry on a wet road. Spray makes it difficult to see. You should

☐ drop back until you can see better

☐ put your headlights on full beam

☐ keep close to the lorry, away from the spray

☐ speed up and overtake quickly

Question 7.19

Mark one answer

You are on a wet motorway with surface spray. You should use

☐ hazard flashers

☐ dipped headlights

☐ rear fog lights

☐ sidelights

Answer

☐ **drop back until you can see better**

In the wet, large vehicles may throw up a lot of spray. This will make it difficult to see ahead. Dropping back further will

• move you out of the spray and so allow you to see further

• increase your separation distance.

It takes longer to stop in the wet and you need to allow more room.

Don't

• get up close behind

• overtake, unless you can see the way ahead is clear.

Answer

☐ **dipped headlights**

When surface spray reduces visibility switch on your dipped headlights. This will help other road users to see you.

Mark one answer

Some two way roads are divided into three lanes. Why are these particularly dangerous?

- Traffic in both directions can use the middle lane to overtake
- Traffic can travel faster in poor weather conditions
- Traffic can overtake on the left
- Traffic uses the middle lane for emergencies only

Answer

- **Traffic in both directions can use the middle lane to overtake**

If you intend to overtake you must consider that approaching traffic could be intending the same manoeuvre. When you have considered the situation and have decided it is safe, indicate your intentions early. This will show the approaching traffic that you intend to pull out.

Mark two answers

Why should you be careful when riding on roads where electric trams operate?

- They cannot steer to avoid you
- They move quickly and quietly
- They are noisy and slow
- They can steer to avoid you
- They give off harmful exhaust fumes

Answers

- **They cannot steer to avoid you**
- **They move quickly and quietly**

Be aware of electric trams. They move silently and quickly and cannot steer to avoid you

Mark one answer

What should you do as you approach this lorry?

- Slow down and be prepared to wait
- Make the lorry wait for you
- Flash your lights at the lorry
- Move to the right hand side of the road

Answer

- **Slow down and be prepared to wait**

Long vehicles may need much more room on the road than other vehicles. They may take up the whole of the road space, so be prepared to give way.

This section looks at the handling of your motorcycle in different conditions

The questions will ask you about

- **Weather conditions**

  be aware of how wet or icy roads will affect the handling of your motorcycle.

- **Road conditions**

  be aware of how the road surface may affect your motorcycle.

- **Time of day**

  be aware of hazards when riding at night.

- **Speed**

  be aware that it's more difficult to control your motorcycle at high speeds.

- **Traffic calming**

  be aware of measures used to slow down traffic where there are pedestrians.

Question 8.1

Mark one answer

To gain basic skills in how to ride a motorcycle you should

- practise off-road with an approved training body
- ride on the road on the first dry day
- practise off-road in a public park or in a quiet cul-de-sac
- ride on the road as soon as possible

Answer

- practise off-road with an approved training body

All new motorcyclists must complete a course of basic training with an approved training body before going on the road. This training is given on a site which has been authorised by the Driving Standards Agency as suitable for off-road training.

Question 8.2

Mark one answer

When you are seated on a stationary motorcycle, your position should allow you to

- just touch the ground with your toes
- place both feet on the ground
- operate the centre stand
- reach the switches by stretching

Answer

- place both feet on the ground

When sitting astride a stationary motorcycle you should be able to place both feet on the ground for maximum control and stability.

Question 8.3

Mark two answers

As a safety measure before starting your engine, you should

- push the motorcycle forward to check the rear wheel turns freely
- engage first gear and apply the rear brake
- engage first gear and apply the front brake
- glance at the neutral light on your instrument panel

Answers

- push the motorcycle forward to check the rear wheel turns freely
- glance at the neutral light on your instrument panel

Before starting the engine you should ensure the motorcycle is in neutral. This can be done by

- moving the motorcycle to see the rear wheel turns freely
- checking the neutral lamp is lit when the ignition is turned on.

Mark one answer

You should not ride with your clutch lever pulled in for longer than necessary because it

☐ increases wear on the gearbox

☐ increases petrol consumption

☐ reduces your control of the motorcycle

☐ reduces the grip of the tyres

Answer

☐ **reduces your control of the motorcycle**

Coasting

- gives you less steering control
- reduces the traction on the road surface
- causes the motorcycle to pick up speed

If you're travelling downhill your motorcycle will gather speed quickly. The engine won't be able to assist the braking.

Mark one answer

You should brake

☐ by using the rear brake first and then the front

☐ when the motorcycle is being turned or ridden through a bend

☐ by pulling in the clutch before using the front brake

☐ when the motorcycle is upright and moving in a straight line

Answer

☐ **when the motorcycle is upright and moving in a straight line**

A motorcycle is most stable when it's upright and moving in a straight line. This is the best time to brake, and normally both brakes should be used, with the front brake being applied just before the rear.

Mark one answer

You are following a vehicle at a safe distance on a wet road. Another driver overtakes you and pulls into the gap you have left. What should you do?

☐ Flash your headlights as a warning

☐ Try to overtake safely as soon as you can

☐ Drop back to regain a safe distance

☐ Stay close to the other vehicle until it moves on

Answer

☐ **Drop back to regain a safe distance**

The weather will affect the way your motorcycle behaves. It will increase the time it takes for you to stop and can affect your control.

Ride at a speed that will allow you to stop safely and in good time.

If another vehicle pulls into the gap you've left, ease back until you've regained your stopping distance. Don't flash your lights or ride up close to it.

Question 8.7

Mark three answers

In which THREE of these situations may you overtake another vehicle on the left?

- When you are in a one-way street
- When approaching a motorway slip road where you will be turning off
- When the vehicle in front is signalling to turn right
- When a slower vehicle is travelling in the right-hand lane of a dual carriageway
- In slow-moving traffic queues when traffic in the right-hand lane is moving more slowly

Answers

- When you are in a one-way street
- When the vehicle in front is signalling to turn right
- In slow-moving traffic queues when traffic in the right-hand lane is moving more slowly

At certain times of the day traffic might be heavy. If traffic is moving in queues and vehicles in the right-hand lane are moving more slowly, you may overtake on the left. Don't keep changing lanes to try and beat the queue.

Question 8.8

Mark one answer

When coming to a normal stop on a motorcycle, you should

- only apply the front brake
- rely just on the rear brake
- apply both brakes smoothly
- apply either of the brakes gently

Answer

- apply both brakes smoothly

In normal riding you should always use both brakes. Harsh or poorly-controlled use of the brakes can cause loss of control and skidding.

Question 8.9

Mark three answers

Which THREE of the following will affect your stopping distance?

- How fast you are going
- The tyres on your vehicle
- The time of day
- The weather
- The street lighting

Answers

- How fast you are going
- The tyres on your vehicle
- The weather

You should be aware that there are several factors that can affect the distance it takes to stop your machine.

Your stopping distance in wet weather will increase. You should double the separation distance from the car in front. Your tyres will have less grip on the road and therefore need more time to stop. Always ride in accordance with the conditions.

Mark one answer

You are travelling in very heavy rain. Your overall stopping distance is likely to be

- doubled
- halved
- up to ten times greater
- no different

Answer

doubled

Apart from the lack of visibility the road will be extremely wet. This will lessen the grip the tyres have on the road and increase the distance it takes to stop. Double your separation distance

Question 8.11

Mark two answers

You are approaching this junction. As the motorcyclist you should

- prepare to slow down
- sound your horn
- keep near the left kerb
- speed up to clear the junction
- stop, as the car has right of way

Answers

prepare to slow down

sound your horn

Look out for road signs indicating side roads, even if you aren't turning off. A driver emerging might not be able to see you due to parked cars or heavy traffic. Always be prepared, and stop if it's necessary. Remember, no one has priority at unmarked crossroads.

Question 8.12

Mark one answer

What can you do to improve your safety on the road as a motorcyclist?

- Anticipate the actions of others
- Stay just above the speed limits
- Keep positioned close to the kerbs
- Remain well below speed limits

Answer

Anticipate the actions of others

Always ride defensively. This means looking and planning ahead as well as anticipating the actions of other road users.

Question 8.13

Mark four answers

Which FOUR types of road surface increase the risk of skidding for motorcyclists?

- White lines
- Dry tarmac
- Tar banding
- Yellow grid lines
- Loose chippings

Answers

- **White lines**
- **Tar banding**
- **Yellow grid lines**
- **Loose chippings**

If you're riding a motorcycle you must look at the road surface ahead. The stability of your motorcycle will depend on it. Also, look out for

- pot-holes
- drain covers (especially in the wet)
- oily surfaces
- road markings
- tram tracks
- wet mud and leaves.

Question 8.14

Mark one answer

You have to brake sharply and your motorcycle starts to skid. You should

- continue braking and select a low gear
- apply the brakes harder for better grip
- select neutral and use the front brake only
- release the brakes and re-apply

Answer

- **release the brakes and re-apply**

If you skid as a result of too much braking you need to

- release the brakes to stop the skid
- re-apply them progressively to stop.

Question 8.15

Mark three answers

Which THREE of these can cause skidding?

- [ ] Braking too gently
- [ ] Leaning too far over when cornering
- [ ] Staying upright when cornering
- [ ] Braking too hard
- [ ] Changing direction suddenly

Answers

- [x] **Leaning too far over when cornering**
- [x] **Braking too hard**
- [x] **Changing direction suddenly**

In order to keep control of your motorcycle and prevent skidding you must plan well ahead to avoid harsh, late braking. Take the road and weather conditions into consideration and ride accordingly.

Question 8.16

Mark two answers

It is very cold and the road looks wet. You cannot hear any road noise. You should

- [ ] continue riding at the same speed
- [ ] ride slower in as high a gear as possible
- [ ] ride in as low a gear as possible
- [ ] keep revving your engine
- [ ] slow down as there may be black ice

Answers

- [x] **ride slower in as high a gear as possible**
- [x] **slow down as there may be black ice**

Rain freezing on roads as it falls is called black ice and isn't clearly visible. The first indication that you might have of it is when the steering becomes very light. You need to keep your speed down and ride according to the weather conditions.

Question 8.17

Mark one answer

You are approaching a road with a surface of loose chippings. What should you do?

- [ ] Ride normally
- [ ] Speed up
- [ ] Slow down
- [ ] Stop suddenly

Answer

- [x] **Slow down**

You should

- ride at an appropriate speed
- apply both front and rear brakes evenly
- brake when travelling in a straight line and your motorcyclee is upright.

Don't make sudden changes of direction unless you are avoiding an accident.

The handling of your motorcycle will be greatly affected by the road surface that you're riding on. Look at the road ahead and be alert if the road looks uneven or has loose chippings. Slow down in good time – braking harshly here will cause you to skid.

DSA THEORY TEST for motorcyclist•

Question 8.18

Mark one answer

Why should you test your brakes after this hazard?

- Because you will be on a slippery road
- Because your brakes will be soaking wet
- Because you will have gone down a long hill
- Because you will have just crossed a long bridge

Question 8.19

Mark one answer

When riding a motorcycle you should wear full protective clothing

- at all times
- only on faster, open roads
- just on long journeys
- only during bad weather

Answer

Because your brakes will be soaking wet

A ford is a crossing over a stream that's shallow enough to ride through. If you've ridden through a ford or a deep puddle the water can affect your brakes. Be sure you check that they're working before returning to normal speed.

Answer

at all times

Protective clothing is designed to protect you from the cold and wet and some kinds of injury.

If you allow yourself to become cold and wet you will lose concentration.

Mark two answers

You have to make a journey in fog. What are the TWO most important things you should do before you set out?

- Fill up with fuel
- Make sure that you have a warm drink with you
- Check that your lights are working
- Check the battery
- Make sure that your visor is clean

Answers

- **Check that your lights are working**
- **Make sure that your visor is clean**

If you're riding a motorcycle, keep your visor as clean as possible to give you a clear view of the road. It's a good idea to carry a clean, damp cloth in a polythene bag for this purpose. When the weather is foggy or misty, ensure that your lights are clean and can be seen clearly by other road users.

Mark one answer

You have to make a journey in foggy conditions. You should

- follow closely other vehicles' tail lights
- avoid using dipped headlights
- leave plenty of time for your journey
- keep two seconds behind other vehicles

Answer

- **leave plenty of time for your journey**

If you're planning to make a journey in foggy conditions listen to the weather reports on the radio or television. Don't ride if visibility is very low or your journey isn't necessary. If you do travel, leave plenty of time for your journey. If there's someone expecting you at the other end of your journey, let them know that you'll be taking longer than normal to arrive. Take your time and don't hurry.

Mark one answer

You are following other vehicles in fog with your lights on. How else can you reduce the chances of being involved in an accident?

- Keep close to the vehicle in front
- Use your main beam instead of dipped headlights
- Keep together with the faster vehicles
- Reduce your speed and increase the gap

Answer

- **Reduce your speed and increase the gap**

Always ensure that you have your lights on and that you're seen by all other road users. Use dipped headlights. If visibility is below 100 metres (328 feet) use fog lights and high-intensity rear lights. Ride at a sensible speed and don't follow the car in front too closely. You'll need to adjust your stopping distance as the road is likely to be wet and slippery.

Question 8.23

Mark one answer

Why should you always reduce your speed when travelling in fog?

- Because the brakes do not work as well
- Because you could be dazzled by other people's fog lights
- Because the engine is colder
- Because it is more difficult to see events ahead

Answer

Because it is more difficult to see events ahead

Riding in fog is hazardous. Only travel if it's really necessary. To ride safely you must always look well ahead. In fog this won't be possible and you'll have less time to react to any hazards. You must reduce your speed.

Question 8.24

Mark one answer

You have to park on the road in fog. You should

- leave sidelights on
- leave dipped headlights and fog lights on
- leave dipped headlights on
- leave main beam headlights on

Answer

leave sidelights on

If you have to park your motorcycle in foggy conditions it's important that it can be seen by other road users.

Try to find a place to park off the road. If this isn't possible leave it facing in the same direction as the traffic. Make sure that your lights are clean and that you leave your sidelights on.

Question 8.25

Mark one answer

The best place to park your motorcycle is

- on soft tarmac
- on bumpy ground
- on grass
- on firm, level ground

Answer

on firm, level ground

Parking your motorcycle on soft ground might cause the stand to sink and the bike to fall over. The ground should also be even and level to ensure that the bike is stable. If possible, park your motorcycle off the road.

Mark one answer

You are on a motorway in fog. The left-hand edge of the motorway can be identified by reflective studs. What colour are they?

■ Green

■ Amber

■ Red

■ White

Answer

■ **Red**

Be especially careful if you're riding on a motorway in fog. You must be able to stop well within the distance that you can see to be clear. Keep in the left-hand lane.

Reflective studs are used on motorways to help you in poor visibility. The studs are coloured so that you'll know which lane you're in and where slip roads join or leave the motorway.

Mark one answer

When riding in windy conditions, you should

■ stay close to large vehicles

■ keep your speed up

■ keep your speed down

■ stay close to the gutter

Answer

■ **keep your speed down**

Strong winds can blow motorcycles off course and even across the road. In windy conditions you need to

• slow down

• avoid riding on exposed roads

• watch for gaps in buildings and hedges where you may be affected by a sudden blast of wind.

Question 8.28

Mark one answer

In normal riding your position on the road should be

about a foot from the kerb

about central in your lane

on the right of your lane

near the centre of the road

Answer

about central in your lane

If you're riding a motorcycle it's very important to ride where other road users can see you. In normal weather you should ride in the centre of your lane. This will

- help you to be seen in the mirror of the vehicle in front
- avoid uneven road surfaces in the gutter
- allow others to overtake on the right if they wish.

Question 8.29

Mark one answer

You are on a motorway at night. You MUST have your headlights switched on unless

there are vehicles close in front of you

you are travelling below 50 mph

the motorway is lit

your motorcycle is broken down on the hard shoulder

Answer

your motorcycle is broken down on the hard shoulder

Always use your headlights at night on a motorway unless you're stopped on the hard shoulder. If you break down and have to stop on the hard shoulder, switch off the main beam. Leave the sidelights on so that other road users can see your motorcycle.

Mark two answers

Which TWO of the following are correct?
When overtaking at night you should

- wait until a bend so that you can see the oncoming headlights
- sound your horn twice before moving out
- be careful because you can see less
- beware of bends in the road ahead
- put headlights on full beam

Answers

- **be careful because you can see less**
- **beware of bends in the road ahead**

Only overtake the vehicle in front if it's really necessary. At night the risks are increased due to the poor visibility. Don't overtake if there's a possibility of

- road junctions
- bends ahead
- the brow of a bridge or hill, except on a dual carriageway
- pedestrian crossings
- double white lines ahead
- vehicles changing direction
- any other potential hazard.

Mark one answer

You are overtaking a car at night. You must be sure that

- you flash your headlights before overtaking
- you select a higher gear
- you have switched your lights to full beam before overtaking
- you do not dazzle other road users

Answer

- **you do not dazzle other road users**

If you wish to overtake at night ensure that your lights don't reflect in the mirror of the car in front. Wait until you've overtaken before switching to full beam.

Mark two answers

When riding at night you should

- wear fluorescent clothing
- ride closer to the vehicle in front
- keep your goggles or visor clean
- ride just left of centre
- use your headlights

Answers

- **keep your goggles or visor clean**
- **use your headlights**

Always make sure that you can see clearly and that other road users can see you. Make sure that your visor or goggles don't have any scratches, which might distort your view or cause dazzle. Wearing bright clothing is a good idea, but remember, only reflective clothing will adequately show up at night.

Question 8.33

Mark one answer

You are parking on a two way road at night. The speed limit is 40 mph. You should park on the

- left with sidelights on
- left with no lights on
- right with sidelights on
- right with dipped headlights on

Answer

■ **left with sidelights on**

On a two way road you may only park at night without lights on

- if the road has a speed limit of 30 mph or less
- you're at least 10 metres (32 feet) away from a junction
- you're facing in the direction of the traffic flow.

Question 8.34

Mark one answer

You are on a narrow road at night. A slower-moving vehicle ahead has been signalling right for some time. What should you do?

- Overtake on the left
- Flash your headlights before overtaking
- Signal right and sound your horn
- Wait for the signal to be cancelled before overtaking

Answer

■ **Wait for the signal to be cancelled before overtaking**

If the vehicle in front has been indicating right for some time, but has made no attempt to turn, wait for the signal to be cancelled. The other driver may have misjudged the distance to the road junction or there might be a hidden hazard.

Mark two answers

A rumble device is designed to

- give directions
- prevent cattle escaping
- alert you to low tyre pressure
- alert you to a hazard
- encourage you to reduce speed

Answers

- **alert you to a hazard**
- **encourage you to reduce speed**

A rumble device is usually raised markings or strips on the road's surface. These strips are in places where traffic has constantly ignored warning or restriction signs. They're there for a good reason. Slow down and be ready to deal with a hazard.

Question 8.36

Mark two answers

Which TWO are correct? The passing places on a single-track road are

- for taking a rest and break
- to pull into if an oncoming vehicle wants to proceed
- for stopping and checking your route
- to turn around in, if you are lost
- to pull into if the car behind wants to overtake

Answers

- **to pull into if an oncoming vehicle wants to proceed**
- **to pull into if the car behind wants to overtake**

If you're riding on a single-track road be prepared to pull over and let other road users pass. There are passing places to enable you to do this, and these shouldn't be used for parking.

Question 8.37

Mark one answer

You see a vehicle coming towards you on a single-track road. You should

- go back to the main road
- do an emergency stop
- stop at a passing place
- put on your hazard warning lights

Answer

- **stop at a passing place**

You must take extra care when riding on single-track roads. You may not be able to see around bends due to high hedges or fences. Ride with caution and expect to meet oncoming vehicles around the next bend. If you do, pull over into or opposite a passing place.

Question 8.38

Mark one answer

Your motorcycle is parked on a two-way road. You should get on from the

- right and apply the rear brake
- left and leave the brakes alone
- left and apply the front brake
- right and leave the brakes alone

Answer

left and apply the front brake

When you get onto a motorcycle you should

- get on from the left side to avoid putting yourself in danger from passing traffic
- apply the front brake to prevent the motorcycle rolling either forwards or backwards.

Question 8.39

Mark one answer

When may you wait in a box junction?

- When you are stationary in a queue of traffic
- When approaching a pelican crossing
- When approaching a zebra crossing
- When oncoming traffic prevents you turning right

Answer

When oncoming traffic prevents you turning right

The purpose of this road marking is to keep the junction clear by preventing traffic from stopping in the path of crossing traffic. If there is already a vehicle waiting to turn right you're free to enter behind it and wait to turn right.

Mark one answer

Which of these plates normally appear with this road sign?

Humps for
½ mile

Hump bridge

Low bridge

Soft verge

Answer

■ Humps for
½ mile

These are in place to slow down the traffic. You should be aware that they are in places where there are often pedestrians, such as

- shopping areas
- near schools
- residential areas.

Watch out for people close to the kerb or crossing the road.

Question 8.41

Mark three answers

How should a scooter be left when parking for some time in a town centre?

■ On firm and level ground

■ By using the side stand leaning over the kerb

■ On the centre stand if fitted

■ Secure and with the fuel tap off

■ On any very wide pavement

Answers

■ On firm and level ground

■ On the centre stand if fitted

■ Secure and with the fuel tap off

When parking a motorcycle always try to park

- on firm level ground
- on the centre stand
- with the fuel tap turned off.

You should always secure your motorcycle using any steering lock or immobiliser fitted by the manufacturer. Any additional visible motorcycle lock that helps to deter thieves is recommended.

Question 8.42

Mark one answer

You are riding along a road which has speed humps. A driver in front is travelling slower than you. You should

- sound your horn
- overtake as soon as you can
- flash your headlights
- slow down and stay behind

Answer

■ **slow down and stay behind**

Normally, you should not overtake other vehicles in traffic-calmed areas. Your speed may exceed that which is safe along that road, so defeating the purpose of the traffic-calming measures.

Question 8.43

Mark two answers

Why should motorcyclists ride carefully where trams operate?

- They do not give way to other traffic
- They do not have mirrors and will not see you
- They do not have lights and might be difficult to see
- The rails could affect your steering and braking

Answers

■ **They do not give way to other traffic**

■ **The rails could affect your steering and braking**

Rails set in the road for trams can affect your steering, especially if they are above the surface of the road or if your front wheel drops into the gap between the road and the rail. They can also present a hazard if you need to brake on them, especially if the roads are wet.

Question 8.44

Mark three answers

Areas reserved for trams may have

- metal studs around them
- white line markings
- zig zag markings
- a different coloured surface
- yellow hatch markings
- a different surface texture

Answers

■ **white line markings**

■ **a different coloured surface**

■ **a different surface texture**

Trams can run on roads used by other vehicles and pedestrians. The area of the road used by the trams is known as the 'swept area'. It should be kept clear, has a coloured surface and is usually edged with white road markings. It might also have a different surface texture.

Mark one answer

It rains after a long dry, hot spell. This may cause the road surface to

- [ ] be unusually slippery
- [ ] give better grip
- [ ] become covered in grit
- [ ] melt and break up

Answer

- [ ] **be unusually slippery**

Roads can become extremely slippery, especially when rain falls onto surfaces that have been subjected to a long, hot, dry spell. Summer showers can be as hazardous as winter frost.

Question 8.46

Mark three answers

The main causes of a motorcycle skidding are

- [ ] heavy and sharp braking
- [ ] excessive acceleration
- [ ] leaning too far when cornering
- [ ] riding in wet weather
- [ ] riding in the winter

Answers

- [ ] **heavy and sharp braking**
- [ ] **excessive acceleration**
- [ ] **leaning too far when cornering**

A good rider tries to avoid skidding. The loss of control during a skid can be lethal.

Question 8.47

Mark one answer

To stop your motorcycle quickly in an emergency you should apply

- [ ] the rear brake only
- [ ] the front brake only
- [ ] the front brake just before the rear
- [ ] the rear brake just before the front

Answer

- [ ] **the front brake just before the rear**

You should plan ahead to avoid the need to stop suddenly. But if an emergency should arise, you must be able to stop safely. Apply the correct amount of braking effort to each wheel.

Question 8.48

Mark one answer

Traffic calming measures are used to

- stop road rage
- help overtaking
- slow traffic down
- help parking

Answer

■ **slow traffic down**

Traffic calming measures are used to make the roads safer for vulnerable road users, such as cyclists, pedestrians and children. These can be designed as chicanes, road humps, etc., to act as obstacles forcing drivers to slow down.

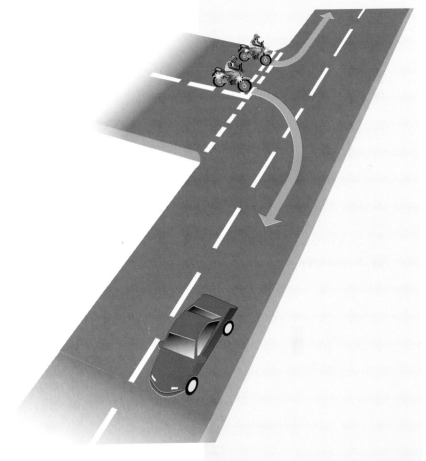

SECTION 9 MOTORWAY RULES

This section looks at motorway rules.

The questions will ask you about

- **Speed limits**

  be aware of the speed restrictions on the motorway.

- **Lane discipline**

  keep to the left lane unless overtaking.

- **Stopping**

  know when and where you can stop on the motorway.

- **Lighting**

  be aware of the importance of being seen.

- **Parking**

  don't stop on the motorway unless in an emergency or you need to due to traffic conditions.

Question 9.1

Mark four answers

Which FOUR of these must NOT use
motorways?

- Learner car drivers
- Motorcycles over 50 cc
- Double-deck buses
- Farm tractors
- Horse riders
- Cyclist

Answers

- Learner car drivers
- Farm tractors
- Horse riders
- Cyclists

In addition, motorways MUST NOT be
used by

- pedestrians
- motorcycles under 50 cc
- certain slow-moving vehicles, without
  permission
- invalid carriages not weighing more than
  254 kg (560 lbs).

Question 9.2

Mark four answers

Which FOUR of these must NOT use
motorways?

- Learner car drivers
- Motorcycles over 50 cc
- Double-deck buses
- Farm tractors
- Learner motorcyclists
- Cyclists

Answers

- Learner car drivers
- Farm tractors
- Learner motorcyclists
- Cyclists

When you've passed your practical driving
test it's a good idea to have some lessons on
motorways. Statistically, motorways are safer
than other roads, but they have rules that
you need to know before you venture out for
the first time. Check with your instructor
about this.

Mark one answer

A motorcycle is not allowed on a motorway if it has an engine size smaller than

- 50 cc
- 125 cc
- 150 cc
- 250 cc

Answer

- **50 cc**

The restricted speed of a small machine will cause a hazard to other motorway users. If you're riding a motorcycle with a small engine, choose another route.

Mark one answer

To ride on a motorway your motorcycle must be

- 50 cc or more
- 100 cc or more
- 125 cc or more
- 250 cc or more

Answer

- **50 cc or more**

Traffic on motorways travels at high speeds. Vehicles need to be capable of keeping up with the flow of traffic. For this reason low-powered vehicles are prohibited.

Mark one answer

Why is it particularly important to carry out a check on your motorcycle before making a long motorway journey?

- You will have to do more harsh braking on motorways
- Motorway service stations do not deal with breakdowns
- The road surface will wear down the tyres faster
- Continuous high speeds may increase the risk of your vehicle breaking down

Answer

- **Continuous high speeds may increase the risk of your motorcycle breaking down**

Before you start your journey make sure that your motorcycle can cope with the demands of high-speed riding. Before starting a motorway journey check your motorcycle's

- oil
- water
- tyres.

Plan your rest stops if you're travelling a long way.

Mark one answer

Immediately after joining a motorway you should normally

- [ ] try to overtake
- [ ] readjust your mirrors
- [ ] position your vehicle in the centre lane
- [ ] keep in the left lane

Answer

- ■ **keep in the left lane**

Give yourself time to get used to the higher speeds of motorway traffic.

Question 9.7

Mark one answer

You are joining a motorway. Why is it important to make full use of the slip road?

- [ ] Because there is space available to turn round if you need to
- [ ] To allow you direct access to the overtaking lanes
- [ ] To build up a speed similar to traffic on the motorway
- [ ] Because you can continue on the hard shoulder

Answer

- ■ **To build up a speed similar to traffic on the motorway**

Try to join the motorway without affecting the progress of the traffic already travelling on it. At busy times this could also mean slowing down to merge into slow-moving traffic.

Question 9.8

Mark one answer

You are joining a motorway from a slip road on the left. You should

- [ ] adjust your speed to the speed of the traffic on the motorway
- [ ] accelerate as quickly as you can and ride straight out
- [ ] ride onto the hard shoulder until a gap appears
- [ ] expect drivers on the motorway to give way to you

Answer

- ■ **adjust your speed to the speed of the traffic on the motorway**

Give way to the traffic already on the motorway and join where there's a suitable gap in the traffic. Try to avoid stopping at the end of the slip road. This might not be avoidable, however, if the motorway is exceptionally busy and there isn't a clear gap in the traffic.

Mark one answer

When joining a motorway you must always

- use the hard shoulder
- stop at the end of the acceleration lane
- come to a stop before joining the motorway
- give way to traffic already on the motorway

Answer

- **give way to traffic already on the motorway**

The traffic may be travelling at high speed, so you should adjust your speed and emerge when it's safe to do so.

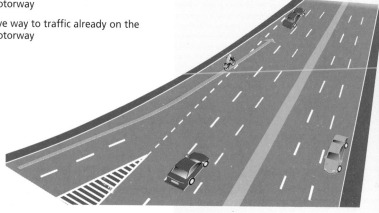

Mark one answer

You are riding on a motorway. Unless signs show otherwise you must NOT exceed

- 50 mph
- 60 mph
- 70 mph
- 80 mph

Answer

- **70 mph**

Ride in accordance with the conditions. Bad weather, heavy traffic or roadworks will limit your speed.

Mark one answer

What is the national speed limit for cars and motorcycles in the centre lane of a three-lane motorway?

- 40 mph
- 50 mph
- 60 mph
- 70 mph

Answer

- **70 mph**

Unless otherwise indicated, the speed limit for the motorway applies to all the lanes. Be on the lookout for any indication of speed limit changes due to roadworks or traffic flow control.

DSA THEORY TEST for motorcyclists

Question 9.12

Mark one answer

What is the national speed limit on motorways for cars and motorcycles?

- 30 mph
- 50 mph
- 60 mph
- 70 mph

Answer

- **70 mph**

Riding at the national speed limit doesn't allow you to hog the outside lane. Always use the nearside or middle lanes whenever possible.

When leaving the motorway, always adjust your speed in good time to deal with

- bends or curves on the slip road
- traffic queuing at roundabouts.

Question 9.13

Mark one answer

On a three-lane motorway which lane should you normally use?

- Left
- Right
- Centre
- Either the right or centre

Answer

- **Left**

On a three-lane motorway you should travel in the left-hand lane unless you're overtaking. This applies regardless of the speed you're travelling at.

Question 9.14

Mark one answer

A basic rule when on motorways is

- use the lane that has least traffic
- keep to the left lane unless overtaking
- overtake on the side that is clearest
- try to keep above 50 mph to prevent congestion

Answer

- **keep to the left lane unless overtaking**

When you've overtaken, move back into the left-hand lane as soon as it's safe to do so. Don't cut across in front of the vehicle that you're overtaking.

Question 9.15

Mark one answer

On a three-lane motorway why should you normally ride in the left lane?

- The left lane is only for lorries and motorcycles
- The left lane should only be used by smaller vehicles
- The lanes on the right are for overtaking
- Motorcycles are not allowed in the far right lane

Answer

■ **The lanes on the right are for overtaking**

Change lanes only if necessary. When you do change lanes observe, signal and manoeuvre in good time. Always remember your 'lifesaver' check. This is a final, quick, rearward glance before you manoeuvre.

Question 9.16

Mark one answer

You are going at 70 mph on a three-lane motorway. There is no traffic ahead. Which lane should you use?

- Any lane
- Middle lane
- Right lane
- Left lane

Answer

■ **Left lane**

Use the left-hand lane if it's free, regardless of the speed you're travelling at.

DSA THEORY TEST for motorcyclists

Question 9.17

Mark one answer

The left-hand lane on a three-lane motorway is for use by

- any vehicle
- large vehicles only
- emergency vehicles only
- slow vehicles only

Question 9.18

Mark one answer

What is the right hand-lane used for on a three-lane motorway?

- Emergency vehicles only
- Overtaking
- Vehicles towing trailers
- Coaches only

Question 9.19

Mark one answer

Which of these IS NOT allowed to travel in the right-hand lane of a three-lane motorway?

- A small delivery van
- A motorcycle
- A vehicle towing a trailer
- A motorcycle and side-car

Answer

any vehicle

On a motorway all traffic should use the left-hand lane unless overtaking. If you need to overtake, use the centre or right-hand lanes.

Make sure that you move back to the left-hand lane when you've finished overtaking. Don't stay in the middle or right-hand lanes if the left-hand lane is free.

Answer

Overtaking

You should keep to the left and only use the right-hand lane if you're passing slower-moving traffic.

Answer

A vehicle towing a trailer

A vehicle with a trailer is restricted to 60 mph. For this reason it isn't allowed in the right-hand lane as it might hold up the faster-moving traffic that wishes to overtake in that lane.

Mark one answer

For what reason may you use the right-hand lane of a motorway?

- For keeping out of the way of lorries
- For riding at more than 70 mph
- For turning right
- For overtaking other vehicles

Answer

For overtaking other vehicles

The right-hand lanes of the motorway are for overtaking. Sometimes you may be directed into a right-hand lane as a result of roadworks or an accident.

Be guided by the signs or police directing the traffic.

Mark one answer

On motorways you should never overtake on the left UNLESS

- you can see well ahead that the hard shoulder is clear
- the traffic in the right-hand lane is signalling right
- you warn drivers behind by signalling left
- there is a queue of traffic to your right that is moving more slowly

Answer

there is a queue of traffic to your right that is moving more slowly

Only overtake on the left if traffic is moving slowly in queues and the traffic on the right is moving slower.

Question 9.22

Mark one answer

On a motorway you may ONLY stop on the hard shoulder

▪ in an emergency

▪ If you feel tired and need to rest

▪ if you accidentally go past the exit that you wanted to take

▪ to pick up a hitchhiker

Answer

▪ **in an emergency**

Don't stop on the hard shoulder to

• have a rest or a picnic
• pick up hitchhikers
• answer a mobile phone
• check a road map.

Never reverse along the hard shoulder if you accidentally go past the exit you wanted.

Question 9.23

Mark two answers

You are travelling on a motorway. You decide you need a rest. You should

▪ stop on the hard shoulder

▪ go to a service area

▪ park on the slip road

▪ park on the central reservation

▪ leave at the next exit

Answers

▪ **go to a service area**

▪ **leave at the next exit**

Stopping on the motorway in any circumstances other than an emergency or traffic queue will cause a major hazard. You should plan your journey so that you have a rest about every two hours.

NI

Mark one answer

You break down on a motorway. You need to call for help. Why may it be better to use an emergency roadside telephone rather than a mobile phone?

▮ It connects you to a local garage

▮ Using a mobile phone will distract other drivers

▮ It allows easy location by the emergency services

▮ Mobile phones do not work on motorways

Answer

▮ **It allows easy location by the emergency services**

On a motorway it is best to use a roadside emergency telephone so that the emergency services are able to locate you easily.

Question 9.26

Mark one answer

The emergency telephones on a motorway are connected to the

▮ ambulance service

▮ police control

▮ fire brigade

▮ breakdown service

Answer

▮ **police control**

The controller will ask you

- the make and colour of your motorcycle
- whether you are a member of an emergency breakdown service
- the number shown on the emergency telephone casing
- whether you are travelling alone.

Question 9.27

Mark one answer

How should you use the emergency telephone on a motorway?

▮ Stay close to the carriageway

▮ Face the oncoming traffic

▮ Keep your back to the traffic

▮ Stand on the hard shoulder

Answer

▮ **Face the oncoming traffic**

Traffic is passing you at speed. The draught from a large lorry could unsteady you, so be prepared. By facing the oncoming traffic you can spot this in advance, as well as other hazards approaching.

DSA THEORY TEST for motorcyclists

Question 9.28

Mark one answer

What should you use the hard shoulder of a motorway for?

▮ Stopping in an emergency

▮ Leaving the motorway

▮ Stopping when you are tired

▮ Joining the motorway

Answer

▮ **Stopping in an emergency**

Don't use the hard shoulder for stopping other than for emergencies. Ride to the next exit or service station if you're able to do so safely.

Question 9.29

Mark one answer

A crawler lane on a motorway is found

▮ on a steep gradient

▮ before a service area

▮ before a junction

▮ along the hard shoulder

Answer

▮ **on a steep gradient**

There are likely to be slow moving large vehicles which might slow down the progress of other traffic. This extra lane is provided for these slow moving vehicles, helping the faster moving traffic to flow. If the crawler lane is free then use it as you would a normal left hand lane.

Question 9.30

Mark three answers

When may you stop on a motorway?

- If you have to read a map
- When you are tired and need a rest
- If red lights show above every lane
- When told to by the police
- If your mobile phone rings
- In an emergency or a breakdown

Answers

- **If red lights show above every lane**
- **When told to by the police**
- **In an emergency or a breakdown**

You may only stop on the carriageway of a motorway

- when told to do so by the police
- when flashing red lights show above every lane
- in a traffic jam
- in an emergency or breakdown.

Question 9.31

Mark one answer

You are allowed to stop on a motorway when you

- need to walk and get fresh air
- wish to pick up hitchhikers
- are told to do so by flashing red lights
- need to use a mobile telephone

Answer

- **are told to do so by flashing red light**

If any of the other lanes show a green arrow you may move into that lane and continue if it is safe to do so. If there are red lights above every lane, you must stop.

Question 9.32

Mark one answer

You are on a motorway. There are red flashing lights above every lane. You must

- pull onto the hard shoulder
- slow down and watch for further signals
- leave at the next exit
- stop and wait

Answer

- **stop and wait**

Flashing red lights above every lane mean you must not go on any further. You'll also see a red cross illuminated. Stop and wait. Don't

- change lanes
- continue
- pull onto the hard shoulder (unless in an emergency).

Mark one answer

You are in the right hand lane on a motorway. You see these overhead signs. This means

- move to the left and reduce your speed to 50 mph

- there are roadworks 50 metres (55 yards) ahead

- use the hard shoulder until you have passed the hazard

- leave the motorway at the next exit

Answer

- **move to the left and reduce your speed to 50 mph**

You must obey this sign. There might not be any visible signs of a problem, but there might be queuing traffic, fog or another hazard ahead.

Mark one answer

When going through a contraflow system on a motorway you should

- ensure that you do not exceed 30 mph

- keep a good distance from the vehicle ahead

- switch lanes to keep the traffic flowing

- stay close to the vehicle ahead to reduce queues

Answer

- **keep a good distance from the vehicle ahead**

There's likely to be a speed restriction in force. Keep to this. Don't

- switch lanes
- drive too close to other traffic.

There will be no permanent barrier between you and the traffic coming towards you. Be extra cautious.

Mark one answer

You are intending to leave the motorway at the next exit. Before you reach the exit you should normally position your motorcycle

▪ in the middle lane

▪ in the left-hand lane

▪ on the hard shoulder

▪ in any lane

Answer

▪ **in the left-hand lane**

You'll see the first sign one mile from the exit. If you're travelling at 60 miles an hour in the right hand-lane you'll only have about 50 seconds before you reach the countdown markers. There's another sign at the half-mile point. Think about what you need to do to be in the left-hand lane in good time. Don't cut across traffic at the last moment.

Mark one answer

What do these motorway signs show?

▪ They are countdown markers to a bridge

▪ They are distance markers to the next telephone

▪ They are countdown markers to the next exit

▪ They warn of a police control ahead

Answer

▪ **They are countdown markers to the next exit**

The exit from a motorway is indicated by countdown markers. These are positioned 90 metres (100 yards) apart, the first being 270 metres (300 yards) from the slip road. Try to get yourself into the left lane in good time.

Question 9.37

Mark one answer

On a motorway the amber reflective studs can be found between

- the hard shoulder and the carriageway
- the acceleration lane and the carriageway
- the central reservation and the carriageway
- each pair of the lanes

Answer

- **the central reservation and the carriageway**

On motorways reflective studs are fitted into the road to help you

- in the dark
- in conditions of poor visibility.

The reflective studs are coloured. These will help you to know which lane you're in and where slip roads join or leave the motorway.

Question 9.38

Mark one answer

What colour are the reflective studs between the lanes on a motorway?

- Green
- Amber
- White
- Red

Answer

- **White**

These are especially useful in bad weather, when visibility is restricted. The light from your headlights is reflected back, highlighting the markings between the lanes.

Mark one answer

You are on a three-lane motorway. There are red reflective studs on your left and white ones to your right. Where are you?

In the right-hand lane

In the middle lane

On the hard shoulder

In the left-hand lane

Answer

In the left-hand lane

The colours of the reflective studs on the motorway and their locations are

- Red – between the hard shoulder and the carriageway.
- White – lane markings.
- Amber – between the edge of the carriageway and the central reserve.
- Green – along slip road exits and entrances.
- Bright Green/Yellow – roadworks and contraflow systems.

Mark one answer

What colour are the reflective studs between a motorway and its slip road?

Amber

White

Green

Red

Answer

Green

These will help you when riding in conditions of poor visibility or in the dark.

 THEORY TEST for motorcyclists

Question 9.41

Mark one answer

You are on a motorway. What colour are the reflective studs on the left of the carriageway?

- Green
- Red
- White
- Amber

Answer

Red

When you have passed your practical test, ask your Instructor about lessons on the motorway. Good professional instruction will help you to become confident and safe on the motorway.

Question 9.42

Mark one answer

You have broken down on a motorway. To find the nearest emergency telephone you should always walk

- with the traffic flow
- facing oncoming traffic
- in the direction shown on the marker posts
- in the direction of the nearest exit

Answer

in the direction shown on the marker posts

Along the hard shoulder there are marker posts at 100 metre intervals. These will direct you to the nearest emergency telephone.

Question 9.43

Mark one answer

You are travelling along the left lane of a three lane motorway. Traffic is joining from a slip road. You should

- race the other vehicles
- move to another lane
- maintain a steady speed
- switch on your hazard flashers

Answer

move to another lane

If it is safe to do so you should move to another lane. This can greatly assist the flow of traffic joining the motorway especially at peak times.

This section looks at rules of the road

The questions will ask you about

- **Speed limits**

  be aware of the speed limits for different types of vehicle.

- **Lane discipline**

  be sure you select the correct lane for the direction you wish to take.

- **Parking**

  choose a sensible place to park.

- **Lighting**

  don't let your motorcycle become a hazard.

Question 10.1

Mark one answer

You are riding slowly in a town centre. Before turning left you should glance over your left shoulder to

- check for cyclists
- help keep your balance
- look for traffic signs
- check for potholes

Answer

check for cyclists

When riding slowly you must remember cyclists. They can travel quickly and fit through surprisingly narrow spaces. Before you turn left in slow moving traffic it's important to check that a cyclist isn't trying to overtake on your left.

Question 10.2

Mark one answer

What is the meaning of this sign?

- Local speed limit applies
- No waiting on the carriageway
- National speed limit applies
- No entry to vehicular traffic

Answer

National speed limit applies

This sign doesn't tell you the speed limit in figures. You should know the speed limit for the type of road that you're on. Study your copy of *The Highway Code*.

Question 10.3

Mark one answer

What is the national speed limit on a single carriageway road for cars and motorcycles?

- 70 mph
- 60 mph
- 50 mph
- 30 mph

Answer

60 mph

Exceeding the speed limit is dangerous and can result in you receiving penalty points on your licence. It isn't worth it. Know the speed limit of the road that you're riding on by observing the road signs.

Mark one answer

What is the national speed limit for cars and motorcycles on a dual carriageway?

- 30 mph
- 50 mph
- 60 mph
- 70 mph

Answer

- **70 mph**

Ensure that you know the speed limit for the road that you're riding on.

The speed limit on a dual carriageway or motorway is 70 mph for cars and motorcycles unless there are signs to indicate otherwise.

The speed limits for different vehicles are listed in *The Highway Code*.

Mark one answer

You are on a road that has no traffic signs. There are street lights. What is the speed limit?

- 20 mph
- 30 mph
- 40 mph
- 60 mph

Answer

- **30 mph**

If you aren't sure of the speed limit it can be indicated by the presence of street lights. If there is street lighting the speed limit will be 30 mph unless otherwise indicated.

Mark one answer

There are no speed limit signs on the road. How is a 30 mph limit indicated?

- By hazard warning lines
- By street lighting
- By pedestrian islands
- By double or single yellow lines

Answer

- **By street lighting**

This usually indicates a 30 mph speed limit when there are no other signs to show other limits.

Question 10.7

Mark one answer

Where you see street lights but no speed limit signs the limit is usually

- 30 mph
- 40 mph
- 50 mph
- 60 mph

Answer

■ **30 mph**

If you are travelling faster than the limit, slow down before you reach the sign.

Check your mirrors and ease off the throttle.

Question 10.8

Mark one answer

What does this sign mean?

- Minimum speed 30 mph
- End of maximum speed
- End of minimum speed
- Maximum speed 30 mph

Answer

■ **End of minimum speed**

A red slash through this sign indicates that the restriction has ended.

Question 10.9

Mark three answers

You are going along a street with parked vehicles on the left-hand side. For which THREE reasons should you keep your speed down?

- So that oncoming traffic can see you more clearly
- You may set off car alarms
- Vehicles may be pulling out
- Drivers' doors may open
- Children may run out from between the vehicles

Answers

■ **Vehicles may be pulling out**

■ **Drivers' doors may open**

■ **Children may run out from between the vehicles**

Care must be taken where there are parked vehicles in a built-up area. Beware of

- vehicles pulling out, especially motorcycles that are small and difficult to see
- pedestrians, especially children, who may run out from between cars
- drivers opening vehicle doors.

Mark one answer

You meet an obstruction on your side of the road. You should

- carry on, you have priority
- give way to oncoming traffic
- wave oncoming vehicles through
- accelerate to get past first

Answer

- **give way to oncoming traffic**

If you have to pass a parked vehicle on your side of the road take care. Give way to oncoming traffic if there isn't enough room for you both to continue safely.

Question 10.11

Mark one answer

There is a tractor ahead of you. You wish to overtake but you are NOT sure if it is safe to do so. You should

- follow another overtaking vehicle through
- sound your horn to the slow vehicle to pull over
- speed through but flash your lights to oncoming traffic
- not overtake if you are in doubt

Answer

- **not overtake if you are in doubt**

Always ask yourself if you really need to overtake. Can you see well down the road? If the answer is no, don't go.

Question 10.12

Mark three answers

Which three of the following are most likely to take an unusual course at roundabouts?

- Horse riders
- Milk floats
- Delivery vans
- Long vehicles
- Estate cars
- Cyclists

Answers

- **Horse riders**
- **Long vehicles**
- **Cyclists**

Long vehicles might have to take a slightly different position when approaching the roundabout or going around it. This is to stop the rear of the vehicle cutting in and mounting the kerb. Horse riders and cyclists might also stay in the left hand lane although they are turning right. Be aware of this and allow them room.

DSA THEORY TEST for motorcyclists

Question 10.13

Mark one answer

You are leaving your motorcycle parked on a road. When may you leave the engine running?

▨ If you will be parked for less than five minutes

▨ If the battery is flat

▨ When in a 20 mph zone

▨ Not on any occasion

Answer

▨ **Not on any occasion**

When you leave your motorcycle parked on a road

• switch off the engine

• lock your motorcycle. Use an anti-theft device if you have one.

Question 10.14

Mark four answers

In which FOUR places must you NOT park or wait?

▨ On a dual carriageway

▨ At a bus stop

▨ On the slope of a hill

▨ Opposite a traffic island

▨ In front of someone else's drive

▨ On the brow of a hill

Answers

▨ **At a bus stop**

▨ **Opposite a traffic island**

▨ **In front of someone else's drive**

▨ **On the brow of a hill**

Care and thought should be taken when parking your own motorcycle. Don't park

• on a footpath, pavement or cycle track

• near a school entrance

• on the approach to a zebra crossing (except in an authorised parking place)

• opposite another parked vehicle.

NI

Question 10.15

Mark one answer

What is the nearest you may park your motorcycle to a junction?

- 10 metres (32 feet)
- 12 metres (39 feet)
- 15 metres (49 feet)
- 20 metres (66 feet)

Answer

- **10 metres (32 feet)**

Don't park within 10 metres (32 feet) of a junction (unless in an authorized parking place) or

- where you would force other traffic to enter a tram lane
- where the kerb has been lowered to help wheelchair users
- in front of an entrance to a property
- where your motorcycle might obstruct a tram.

Question 10.16

Mark two answers

In which TWO places must you NOT park?

- Near a school entrance
- Near a police station
- In a side road
- At a bus stop
- In a one-way street

Answers

- **Near a school entrance**
- **At a bus stop**

It may be tempting to park where you shouldn't while you run a quick errand. Careless parking is a selfish act and could endanger other road users.

NI

Question 10.17

Mark three answers

In which THREE places must you NOT park your motorcycle?

- Near the brow of a hill
- At or near a bus stop
- Where there is no pavement
- Within 10 metres (32 feet) of a junction
- On a 40 mph road

Answers

- **Near the brow of a hill**
- **At or near a bus stop**
- **Within 10 metres (32 feet) of a junction**

Other traffic will have to pull out to pass you. This might mean they have to use the other side of the road where there might be oncoming traffic.

Parking near a junction could restrict the view for emerging vehicles.

Question 10.18

Mark one answer

On a clearway you must not stop

- at any time
- when it is busy
- in the rush hour
- during daylight hours

Answer

- **at any time**

Clearways are in place so that traffic can flow without the obstruction of parked vehicles. Just one parked vehicle will cause an obstruction for all other traffic. You should not even stop to pick up or set down passengers.

Question 10.19

Mark one answer

What is the meaning of this sign?

- No entry
- Waiting restrictions
- National speed limit
- School crossing patrol

Answer

- **Waiting restrictions**

Don't cause an obstruction by stopping or waiting where there are restrictions. You should know the meaning of road signs. Buy a copy of *Know Your Traffic Signs* (The Stationery Office) and study it.

Question 10.20

Mark one answer

You are looking for somewhere to park your motorcycle. The area is full EXCEPT for spaces marked 'disabled use'. You can

- use these spaces when elsewhere is full
- park if you stay with your motorcycle
- use these spaces, disabled or not
- not park there unless permitted

Answer

- **not park there unless permitted**

Don't be selfish. Find somewhere else to park, even if it means that you have to walk further.

Mark one answer

Your motorcycle is parked on the road at night. When must you use sidelights?

- [ ] Where there are continuous white lines in the middle of the road
- [ ] Where the speed limit exceeds 30 mph
- [ ] Where you are facing oncoming traffic
- [ ] Where you are near a bus stop

Answer

- [ ] **Where the speed limit exceeds 30 mph**

When parking at night, park in the direction of the traffic. This will enable other road users to see the reflectors on the rear of your motorcycle.

Use your parking lights if the speed limit is over 30 mph.

Mark one answer

You park overnight on a road with a 40 mph speed limit. You should

- [ ] park facing the traffic
- [ ] park with sidelights on
- [ ] park with dipped headlights on
- [ ] park near a street light

Answer

- [ ] **park with sidelights on**

Make sure that other road users can see your machine. Park in the direction of the traffic flow so that your motorcycle isn't mistaken for a moving oncoming car.

Mark one answer

You can park on the right-hand side of a road at night

- [ ] in a one-way street
- [ ] with your sidelights on
- [ ] more than 10 metres (32 feet) from a junction
- [ ] under a lamp-post

Answer

- [ ] **in a one-way street**

Motorcycles are fitted with red rear reflectors that show up when headlights shine on them. These are useful when you are parked at night, but will only reflect if your motorcycle is parked in the same direction as the traffic passing alongside. Normally you should park on the left, but if you're in a one-way street the right-hand side is OK too.

Question 10.24

Mark one answer

On a three-lane dual carriageway the right-hand lane can be used for

- overtaking only, never turning right
- overtaking or turning right
- fast-moving traffic only
- turning right only, never overtaking

Answer

■ overtaking or turning right

Use the left-hand lane at other times. When overtaking on a dual carriageway be on the lookout for vehicles ahead that are turning right. They're likely to be slowing or stopped. You need to see them in good time so that you can take appropriate action.

Question 10.25

Mark one answer

You are riding on a busy dual carriageway. When changing lanes you should

- rely totally on mirrors
- always increase your speed
- signal so others will give way
- use mirrors and shoulder checks

Answer

■ use mirrors and shoulder checks

Before you change lanes you need to see if there's a safe gap to move across into. You have areas behind and to the side which are not covered by the mirrors. As well as using your mirrors you need to make a shoulder check to see if any vehicle is in this blind area before changing direction.

Question 10.26

Mark two answers

You are on a two-lane dual carriageway. For which TWO of the following would you use the right-hand lane?

- Turning right
- Normal progress
- Staying at the minimum allowed speed
- Constant high speed
- Overtaking slower traffic
- Mending punctures

Answers

- **Turning right**
- **Overtaking slower traffic**

If you overtake on a dual carriageway move back into the left lane as soon as it's safe. Don't cut in across the path of the vehicle you've just passed.

Question 10.27

Mark one answer

You are entering an area of roadworks. There is a temporary speed limit displayed. You must

- not exceed the speed limit
- obey the limit only during rush hour
- accept the speed limit as advisable
- obey the limit except for overnight

Answer

- **not exceed the speed limit**

Where there are extra hazards, such as roadworks, it's often necessary to slow traffic down by imposing a temporary speed limit. These speed limits aren't just advisory – they must be adhered to.

Question 10.28

Mark two answers

As a motorcycle rider which TWO lanes must you NOT use?

- Crawler lane
- Overtaking lane
- Acceleration lane
- Cycle lane
- Tram lane

Answers

- **Cycle lane**
- **Tram lane**

In some towns motorcycles are permitted to use bus lanes. Check the signs carefully.

DSA THEORY TEST for motorcyclists

Question 10.29

Mark one answer

You are approaching a busy junction. There are several lanes with road markings. At the last moment you realise that you are in the wrong lane. You should

- continue in that lane
- force your way across
- stop until the area has cleared
- use clear arm signals to cut across

Answer

continue in that lane

There are times where road markings can be obscured by queuing traffic, or you might be unsure of your correct lane. Don't cut across lanes or bully other drivers to let you in. Follow the lane you're in and find somewhere safe to turn around if you need to.

Question 10.30

Mark one answer

Where may you overtake on a one-way street?

- Only on the left-hand side
- Overtaking is not allowed
- Only on the right-hand side
- Either on the right or the left

Answer

Either on the right or the left

You can overtake other traffic on either side when travelling in a one-way street. Make full use of your mirrors and ensure that it's clear all around before you attempt to overtake. Look for signs and road markings and use the most suitable lane for your destination.

Question 10.31

Mark one answer

You are going along a single-track road with passing places only on the right. The driver behind wishes to overtake. You should

- speed up to get away from the following driver
- switch on your hazard warning lights
- wait opposite a passing place on your right
- pull into a passing place on your right

Answer

wait opposite a passing place on your right

Some roads are only wide enough for one vehicle. Often this type of road has special passing places where the road is widened for a short distance.

If there's a car coming toward you pull into a passing place on your left or stop opposite one on your right. Don't

- force other vehicles to reverse
- pull into the passing place on the right.

Question 10.32

Mark two answers

You are on a road that is only wide enough for one vehicle. There is a car coming towards you. Which TWO of these would be correct?

- [ ] Pull into a passing place on your right
- [ ] Force the other driver to reverse
- [x] Pull into a passing place if your motorcycle is wider
- [ ] Pull into a passing place on your left
- [ ] Wait opposite a passing place on your right
- [ ] Wait opposite a passing place on your left

Answers

- [x] Pull into a passing place on your left
- [x] Wait opposite a passing place on your right

If you meet another vehicle in a narrow road and the passing place is on the right, pull up opposite it. This will allow the oncoming vehicle to pull into it and pass you safely.

Question 10.33

Mark one answer

Signals are normally given by direction indicators and

- [ ] brake lights
- [ ] side lights
- [ ] fog lights
- [ ] interior lights

Answer

- [ ] brake lights

Your brake lights will give an indication to traffic behind that you're slowing down. Good anticipation will allow you time to check your mirrors before slowing.

If you're intending to change direction you should use your direction indicators before you brake.

Question 10.34

Mark one answer

When going straight ahead at a roundabout you should

- [ ] indicate left before leaving the roundabout
- [ ] not indicate at any time
- [ ] indicate right when approaching the roundabout
- [ ] indicate left when approaching the roundabout

Answer

- [ ] indicate left before leaving the roundabout

When you want to go ahead at a roundabout indicate left just after you pass the exit before the one you wish to take. Don't

- signal right on approach
- signal left on approach.

Question 10.35

Mark one answer

Which vehicle might have to use a different course to normal at roundabouts?

- Sports car
- Van
- Estate car
- Long vehicle

Answer

Long vehicle

A long vehicle may have to straddle lanes either on or approaching a roundabout so that the rear wheels don't cut in over the kerb. Stay well back and give it room.

Question 10.36

Mark one answer

You are going straight ahead at a roundabout. How should you signal?

- Signal right on the approach and then left to leave the roundabout
- Signal left as you leave the roundabout
- Signal left on the approach to the roundabout and keep the signal on until you leave
- Signal left just after you pass the exit before the one you will take

Answer

Signal left just after you pass the exit before the one you will take

To go straight ahead at a roundabout you should normally approach in the left-hand lane. Where there are road markings, use the lane indicated.

Ensure that you signal correctly and in good time. Other road users need to know your intentions.

Question 10.37

Mark one answer

You are turning right at a large roundabout. Just before you leave the roundabout you should

- take a 'lifesaver' glance over your left shoulder
- take a 'lifesaver' glance over your right shoulder
- put on your right indicator
- cancel the left indicator

Answer

take a 'lifesaver' glance over your left shoulder

You must be aware of what's happening behind and alongside you. A final, quick rearward glance will give you the chance to react if it isn't safe to make the manoeuvre.

Mark one answer

At a crossroads there are no signs or road markings. Two vehicles approach. Which has priority?

- [ ] Neither vehicle
- [ ] The vehicle travelling the fastest
- [ ] The vehicle on the widest road
- [ ] Vehicles approaching from the right

Answer

■ **Neither vehicle**

At a crossroads where there are no GIVE WAY signs or road markings BE VERY CAREFUL. No vehicle has priority, even if the size of the roads are different.

Mark one answer

Who has priority at an unmarked crossroads?

- [ ] The larger vehicle
- [ ] No one has priority
- [ ] The faster vehicle
- [ ] The smaller vehicle

Answer

■ **No one has priority**

Practise good observation in all directions before you emerge or make a turn.

Question 10.40

Mark three answers

When filtering through slow moving or stationary traffic you should

- watch for hidden vehicles emerging from side roads
- continually use your horn as a warning
- look for vehicles changing course suddenly
- always ride with your hazard lights on
- stand up on the footrests for a good view ahead
- look for pedestrians walking between vehicles

Answers

- **watch for hidden vehicles emerging from side roads**
- **look for vehicles changing course suddenly**
- **look for pedestrians walking between vehicles**

Other road users may not expect or look for motorcycles filtering through slow moving or stationary traffic. The view all around will be reduced by the vehicles and you will need to watch for

- pedestrians walking between the vehicles
- vehicles suddenly changing direction
- vehicles pulling out of side roads.

Question 10.41

Mark one answer

You are intending to turn right at a crossroads. An oncoming driver is also turning right. It will normally be safer to

- keep the other vehicle to your RIGHT and turn behind it (offside to offside)
- keep the other vehicle to your LEFT and turn in front of it (nearside to nearside)
- carry on and turn at the next junction instead
- hold back and wait for the other driver to turn first

Answer

- **keep the other vehicle to your RIGHT and turn behind it (offside to offside)**

At some junctions the layout may make it difficult to turn this way. Be prepared to pass nearside to nearside, but take extra care. Your view ahead will be obscured by the vehicle turning in front of you.

Mark one answer

You are both turning right at these crossroads. It is safer to keep the car to your right so you can

▨ see approaching traffic

▨ keep close to the kerb

▨ keep clear of following traffic

▨ make oncoming vehicles stop

Answer

▨ **see approaching traffic**

When turning right at this crossroads you should keep the oncoming car on your right. This will give you a clear view of the road ahead and any oncoming traffic.

Mark one answer

The dual carriageway you are turning right onto has a narrow central reserve. You should

▨ proceed to central reserve and wait

▨ wait until the road is clear in both directions

▨ stop in first lane so that other vehicles give way

▨ emerge slightly to show your intentions

Answer

▨ **wait until the road is clear in both directions**

If you treat this carriageway as two separate roads you could cause an obstruction to traffic in both directions.

Question 10.44

Mark one answer

You may only enter a box junction when

- there are less than two vehicles in front of you
- the traffic lights show green
- your exit road is clear
- you need to turn left

Answer

☐ **your exit road is clear**

Box junctions are marked on the road to prevent the road becoming blocked.

Don't enter the box unless your exit road is clear. You may only wait in the box if your exit road is clear but oncoming traffic is preventing you from completing the turn.

Question 10.45

Mark one answer

You may wait in a yellow box junction when

- oncoming traffic is preventing you from turning right
- you are in a queue of traffic turning left
- you are in a queue of traffic to go ahead
- you are on a roundabout

Answer

☐ **oncoming traffic is preventing you from turning right**

The purpose of this road marking is to keep the centre of the junction clear of queuing traffic when the lights change priority. Don't stop in it if you aren't turning right.

Question 10.46

Mark three answers

On which THREE occasions MUST you stop your motorcycle?

- When involved in an accident
- At a red traffic light
- When signalled to do so by a police officer
- At a junction with double broken white lines
- At a pelican crossing when the amber light is flashing and no pedestrians are crossing

Answers

- When involved in an accident
- At a red traffic light
- When signalled to do so by a police officer

Don't stop or hold up traffic unnecessarily. However you MUST stop when signalled to do so by

- a police officer
- a school crossing patrol
- a red traffic light

or when you have had an accident.

Question 10.47

Mark three answers

You MUST stop when signalled to do so by which THREE of these?

- A police officer
- A pedestrian
- A school crossing patrol
- A bus driver
- A red traffic light

Answers

- A police officer
- A school crossing patrol
- A red traffic light

Looking well ahead and 'reading' the road will help you to anticipate hazards. This will allow you to stop safely if asked to do so by a person or a road sign.

Question 10.48

Mark three answers

At roadworks which of the following can control traffic flow?

- A STOP–GO board
- Flashing amber lights
- A policeman
- Flashing red lights
- Temporary traffic lights

Answers

- A STOP–GO board
- A policeman
- Temporary traffic lights

As you approach the warning signs you should be considering what actions you need to take. You might have to slow right down or stop. Obey any instructions you are given and don't try to beat any lights by riding up to them quickly.

Question 10.49

Mark one answer

You are waiting at a level crossing. A train has passed but the lights keep flashing. You must

- carry on waiting
- phone the signal operator
- edge over the stop line and look for trains
- park your motorcycle and investigate

Answer

■ **carry on waiting**

If the lights at a level crossing continue to flash after a train has passed, wait, there might be another train coming. Time seems to pass slowly when you're held up in a queue. Be patient and wait until the lights stop flashing.

Question 10.50

Mark one answer

You will see these markers when approaching

- the end of a motorway
- a concealed level crossing
- a concealed speed limit sign
- the end of a dual carriageway

Answer

■ **a concealed level crossing**

There may be a bend before a level crossing, in which case you won't be able to see barriers or waiting traffic ahead. These signs give you an early warning that you may find these hazards just around the bend.

Mark one answer

Someone is waiting to cross at a zebra crossing. They are standing on the pavement. You should normally

- go on quickly before they step onto the crossing

- stop before you reach the zigzag lines and let them cross

- stop, let them cross, wait patiently

- ignore them as they are still on the pavement

Answer

■ **stop, let them cross, wait patiently**

The pedestrian is showing an intention to cross. If you are looking well down the road you will give yourself enough time to slow down and stop correctly. Don't forget to check your mirrors before slowing down.

Mark one answer

At toucan crossings, apart from pedestrians you should be aware of

- emergency vehicles emerging

- buses pulling out

- trams crossing in front

- cyclists riding across

Answer

■ **cyclists riding across**

The use of cycles is being encouraged and more toucan crossings are being installed. These crossings enable pedestrians and cyclists to cross the path of other traffic. Watch out, as cyclists will approach the crossing faster than a pedestrian.

Question 10.53

Mark two answers

Who can use a toucan crossing?

- Trains
- Cyclists
- Buses
- Pedestrians
- Trams

Answers

- **Cyclists**
- **Pedestrians**

Toucan crossings are similar to pelican crossings. Cyclists share the crossing with pedestrians without the need to dismount. They're shown a green cycle when it's safe to cross.

Question 10.54

Mark one answer

At a pelican crossing, what does a flashing amber light mean?

- You must not move off until the lights stop flashing
- You must give way to pedestrians still on the crossing
- You can move off, even if pedestrians are still on the crossing
- You must stop because the lights are about to change to red

Answer

- **You must give way to pedestrians still on the crossing**

If the road is clear then proceed. The green light will show after the flashing amber.

Question 10.55

Mark one answer

You want to tow a trailer with your motorcycle. Your engine must be more than

- 50cc
- 125cc
- 525cc
- 1000cc

Answer

- **125cc**

You must remember that towing a trailer requires special care. You must obey the speed limit restrictions which apply to all vehicles towing trailers.

DO NOT FORGET IT IS THERE.

Mark one answer

What is the national speed limit on a single carriageway?

■ 40mph

■ 50mph

■ 60mph

■ 70mph

Answer

■ **60mph**

You don't have to ride up to the speed limit. Use your own judgement and ride at a speed that suits the prevailing road and traffic conditions.

Mark one answer

What does this sign mean?

■ No parking for solo motorcycles

■ Parking for solo motorcycles

■ Passing place for motorcycles

■ Police motorcycles only

Answer

■ **Parking for solo motorcycles**

In some towns and cities there are special areas reserved for the parking of motorcycles Look out for these signs.

Mark three answers

Your motorcycle will be parked for a long time. You should

■ use the centre stand if fitted

■ park on a wide pavement

■ lean it against a wall

■ switch off the fuel tap

■ park where the ground is firm and level

■ park with your lights on in daytime

Answers

■ **use the centre stand if fitted**

■ **switch off the fuel tap**

■ **park where the ground is firm and level**

Park on firm and level ground. Your centre stand, if fitted, will give greater stability. Don't forget to switch off your fuel tap where necessary and take the ignition key with you.

Question 10.59

Mark one answer

You are riding towards road works. The temporary traffic lights are at red. The road ahead is clear. What should you do?

- Ride on with extreme caution
- Ride on at normal speed
- Carry on if approaching cars have stopped
- Wait for the green light

Answer

Wait for the green light

You must obey all traffic signs. Just because the lights are temporary it does not mean that you can disregard them.

Question 10.60

Mark one answer

You are travelling on a well lit road at night in a built up area. By using dipped headlights you will be able to

- see further along the road
- go at a much faster speed
- switch to main beam quickly
- be easily seen by others

Answer

be easily seen by others

Travelling on a well lit road you may still be difficult to see. Dipped headlights will make you more conspicuous than if you use only sidelights.

Question 10.61

Mark one answer

When can you park on the left opposite these road markings?

- If the line nearest to you is broken
- When there are no yellow lines
- To pick up or set down passengers
- During daylight hours only

Answer

To pick up or set down passengers

You must not park or stop on a road marked with double white lines, except to pick up or set down passengers.

This section looks at road and traffic signs.

The questions will ask you about

- **Road signs**

  these tell you about the road ahead.

- **Speed limits**

  recognise signs showing speed limits.

- **Road markings**

  be aware that directions might be painted on the road surface.

- **Regulations**

  these can be shown to you by means of a road sign.

Question 11.1

Mark one answer

You MUST obey signs giving orders. These signs are mostly in

- green rectangles
- red triangles
- blue rectangles
- red circles

Answer

- **red circles**

Traffic signs can be divided into three classes – those giving orders, those warning and those informing. On the road each class of sign has a different shape.

Question 11.2

Mark one answer

Traffic signs giving orders are generally which shape?

Answer

Road signs in the shape of a circle give orders. Those with a red circle are mostly prohibitive. The stop sign is octagonal to give it greater prominence. These signs must always be obeyed.

Question 11.3

Mark one answer

Which type of sign tells you NOT to do something?

Answer

Signs in the shape of a circle mean that you aren't allowed to do something. Study *Know Your Traffic Signs* (The Stationery Office) to ensure that you understand the order you're shown.

Question 11.4

Mark one answer

What does this sign mean?

- Maximum speed limit with traffic calming
- Minimum speed limit with traffic calming
- '20 cars only' parking zone
- Only 20 cars allowed at any one time

Answer

Maximum speed limit with traffic calming

If you're riding in areas where there are likely to be pedestrians such as

- outside schools
- near parks
- residential areas
- shopping areas

be extra cautious and keep your speed down. Many local authorities have taken measures to slow traffic down by creating traffic calming measures such as speed humps. They're there for a reason: slow down.

Question 11.5

Mark one answer

Which sign means no motor vehicles are allowed?

Answer

Certain areas are set aside for pedestrians to walk free of traffic.

Question 11.6

Mark one answer

Which of these signs means no motor vehicles?

Answer

If you are driving a motor vehicle or riding a motorcycle you must not enter. This area has been especially designated for pedestrians.

Question 11.7

Mark one answer

What does this sign mean?

New speed limit 20 mph

No vehicles over 30 tonnes

Minimum speed limit 30 mph

End of 20 mph zone

Answer

End of 20 mph zone

Where you see this sign the 20 mph restriction ends. Only increase your speed if it's safe to do so. Check all around and well down the road before increasing your speed.

Mark one answer

This traffic sign means there is

- a compulsory maximum speed limit

- an advisory maximum speed limit

- a compulsory minimum speed limit

- an advised separation distance

Answer

■ **a compulsory maximum speed limit**

In this picture the traffic is slow moving, which could be due to road works or other temporary obstruction. The sign gives you a early warning of a speed restriction. If you are travelling at a higher speed, slow down good time.

Mark one answer

What does this sign mean?

- No overtaking

- No motor vehicles

- Clearway (no stopping)

- Cars and motorcycles only

Answer

■ **No motor vehicles**

Traffic may be prohibited from certain roads A sign will indicate which types of vehicles aren't allowed to use it. Make sure that you know which signs apply to the vehicle you're using.

Mark one answer

What does this sign mean?

- No parking

- No road markings

- No through road

- No entry

Answer

■ **No entry**

Not knowing the meaning of a road sign could lead you into a dangerous situation.

DSA THEORY TEST **for motorcyclist**

Question 11.11

Mark one answer

What does this sign mean?

☐ Bend to the right

☐ Road on the right closed

☐ No traffic from the right

☐ No right turn

Answer

☐ **No right turn**

The road on the right might be a no entry or the sign could be there to allow the traffic on the main road to flow by stopping cars queuing to turn right.

Question 11.12

Mark one answer

Which sign means 'no entry'?

Answer

Look out for traffic signs as you ride. Disobeying or not seeing a sign could not only be dangerous, but also an offence; you could be fined.

Mark one answer

What does this sign mean?

- Route for trams only
- Route for buses only
- Parking for buses only
- Parking for trams only

Answer

Route for trams only

Avoid blocking tram routes. Trams are fixed on their route and can't dodge around other vehicles and pedestrians. Modern trams travel quickly and are quiet so you might not hear them approaching.

Mark one answer

Which type of vehicle does this sign apply to?

- Wide vehicles
- Long vehicles
- High vehicles
- Heavy vehicles

Answer

High vehicles

The triangular shapes at the top and bottom of the sign mean that the sign is showing you the restricted height.

Question 11.15

Mark one answer

Which sign means NO motor vehicles allowed?

Answer

This sign is used to enable pedestrians to walk free from traffic. It's often found in shopping areas.

Question 11.16

Mark one answer

What does this sign mean?

- You have priority
- No motor vehicles
- Two-way traffic
- No overtaking

Answer

No overtaking

Road signs that show no overtaking will be placed in locations where passing the vehicle in front is dangerous. If you see this sign don't attempt to overtake. The sign is there for a reason and you must obey it.

Mark one answer

What does this sign mean?

Keep in one lane

Give way to oncoming traffic

Do not overtake

Form two lanes

Answer

Do not overtake

If you're behind a slow-moving vehicle, be patient. Wait until the restriction no longer applies and you can overtake safely.

Mark one answer

Which sign means no overtaking?

Answer

This sign indicates that overtaking here would be dangerous. Don't take risks.

Mark one answer

What does this sign mean?

Waiting restrictions apply

Waiting permitted

National speed limit applies

Clearway (no stopping)

Answer

Waiting restrictions apply

There will be a plate or additional sign to tell you when the restrictions apply.

DSA THEORY TEST for motorcyclist

Mark one answer

What does this sign mean?

- You can park on the days and times shown
- No parking on the days and times shown
- No parking at all from Monday to Friday
- You can park at any time; the urban clearway ends

Answer

■ **No parking on the days and times shown**

Before you leave your motorcycle parked at the side of the road check that the space isn't restricted. Parking times vary from place to place, so always check the sign before securing and leaving your motorcycle.

Mark one answer

What does this sign mean?

- End of restricted speed area
- End of restricted parking area
- End of clearway
- End of cycle route

Answer

■ **End of restricted parking area**

Even though there are no restrictions, make sure that you park where you won't cause an obstruction or endanger other road users.

Question 11.22

Mark one answer

Which sign means 'no stopping'?

Answer

Stopping where you see this sign is likely to cause congestion. Allow the traffic to flow by obeying the signs.

Question 11.23

Mark one answer

What does this sign mean?

- [ ] Roundabout
- [ ] Crossroads
- [ ] No stopping
- [ ] No entry

Answer

No stopping

This sign is in place to ensure a clear route for traffic. Don't stop except in an emergency

Question 11.24

Mark one answer

You see this sign ahead. It means

- [ ] national speed limit applies
- [ ] waiting restrictions apply
- [ ] no stopping
- [ ] no entry

Answer

no stopping

There are stretches of road where you aren't allowed to stop (unless in an emergency). These are called 'clearways'. You'll see this sign. Stopping where these restrictions apply may be dangerous and could cause an obstruction. Restrictions might apply for several miles and this may be indicated on the sign.

DSA THEORY TEST for motorcyclists

Question 11.25

Mark one answer

What does this sign mean?

- Distance to parking place ahead
- Distance to public telephone ahead
- Distance to public house ahead
- Distance to passing place ahead

Answer

Distance to parking place ahead

If you intend to stop and rest note this early indication.

Question 11.26

Mark one answer

What does this sign mean?

- Vehicles may not park on the verge or footway
- Vehicles may park on the left-hand side of the road only
- Vehicles may park fully on the verge or footway
- Vehicles may park on the right-hand side of the road only

Answer

Vehicles may park fully on the verge or footway

In order to keep roads free from parked cars there are some areas where you're allowed to park on the verge. Only do this where you see the sign. Parking on verges or kerbs in other areas could lead to a fine.

Mark one answer
What does this traffic sign mean?

No overtaking allowed

Give priority to oncoming traffic

Two way traffic

One-way traffic only

Answer

Give priority to oncoming traffic

Priority signs are normally shown where the road is narrow and there isn't enough room for two vehicles to pass, such as

- a narrow bridge
- at roadworks
- a width restriction.

Make sure that you know who has priority. Comply with the sign and don't force your way through. Show courtesy and consideration to other road users.

Mark one answer
What is the meaning of this traffic sign?

End of two-way road

Give priority to vehicles coming towards you

You have priority over vehicles coming towards you

Bus lane ahead

Answer

You have priority over vehicles coming towards you

Don't force your way through. Show courtesy and consideration to other road users. Although you have priority, make sure oncoming traffic is going to give way.

Question 11.29

Mark one answer

Which sign means 'traffic has priority over oncoming vehicles'?

Answer

Even though you may have priority, give way if proceeding is likely to cause an accident, congestion or confrontation.

Question 11.30

Mark one answer

What MUST you do when you see this sign?

Stop, ONLY if traffic is approaching

Stop, even if the road is clear

Stop, ONLY if children are waiting to cross

Stop, ONLY if a red light is showing

Answer

Stop, even if the road is clear

A stop sign is shown on an octagonal-shaped background. The sign will be at a junction where visibility is restricted or there's heavy traffic.

IT MUST BE OBEYED. YOU MUST STOP.

Practice good all-round observation before moving off.

Mark one answer

What does this sign mean?

No overtaking

You are entering a one-way street

Two-way traffic ahead

You have priority over vehicles from the opposite direction

Answer

You have priority over vehicles from the opposite direction

Don't force the issue. Slow down and give way to avoid confrontation or an accident.

Question 11.32

Mark one answer

What shape is a STOP sign at a junction?

Answer

The STOP sign is distinctive and the only sign of this shape. You must stop and make effective observation before proceeding.

Question 11.33

Mark one answer

At a junction you see this sign partly covered by snow. What does it mean?

Cross roads

Give way

Stop

Turn right

Answer

 Stop

The STOP sign is the only sign this shape. This is to give it greater prominence. Although the snow has covered the wording, you must still be able to recognise and obey this sign.

Question 11.34

Mark one answer

Which shape is used for a GIVE WAY sign?

Answer

Other warning signs are the same shape and colour, but the GIVE WAY sign points downwards. You must give way to traffic already on the major road.

Question 11.35

Mark one answer

What does this sign mean?

- Service area 30 miles ahead
- Maximum speed 30 mph
- Minimum speed 30 mph
- Lay-by 30 miles ahead

Answer

■ **Minimum speed 30 mph**

This sign is shown where slow-moving vehicles would impede the flow of traffic. However, if you need to slow down to avoid a potential accident you should do so.

Mark one answer

Which of these signs means turn left ahead?

Answer

This sign gives a clear instruction. You should be looking out for signs as you ride. Prepare to negotiate a left-hand turn.

Mark one answer

At a mini-roundabout you should

give way to traffic from the right

give way to traffic from the left

give way to traffic from the other way

stop even when clear

Answer

give way to traffic from the right

Look out for other traffic as you approach. Vehicles entering the mini-roundabout from your left or ahead might prevent traffic on your right from proceeding. Watch for their signals and continue if it's safe to do so.

Mark one answer

What does this sign mean?

Buses turning

Ring road

Mini roundabout

Keep right

Answer

Mini-roundabout

Look out for any direction signs and judge whether you need to signal your intentions. Do this in good time so that other road users approaching the roundabout can assess the situation.

DSA THEORY TEST for motorcyclists

Question 11.39

Mark one answer
What does this sign mean?

Give way to oncoming vehicles

Approaching traffic passes you on both sides

Turn off at the next available junction

Pass either side to get to the same destination

Answer

Pass either side to get to the same destination

These signs are often seen in one-way streets that have more than one lane. Use the route that's the most convenient and doesn't require a late change of direction.

Question 11.40

Mark one answer
What does this sign mean?

Route for trams

Give way to trams

Route for buses

Give way to buses

Answer

Route for trams

Take extra care when you first encounter trams. Look out for road markings and signs that alert you to them. Modern trams are very quiet and you may not hear them approaching.

Mark one answer

What does a circular traffic sign with a blue background do?

Give warning of a motorway ahead

Give directions to a car park

Give motorway information

Give an instruction

Answer

Give an instruction

Signs with blue circles give a positive instruction. They will often be seen in towns or urban areas. For example mini-roundabout or pass either side.

Mark one answer

Which of these signs means that you are entering a one-way street?

Answer

If the road has two lanes you can use either lane and overtake on either side. Use the lane that's more convenient for your destination.

Mark one answer

Where would you see a contraflow bus and cycle lane?

On a dual carriageway

On a roundabout

On an urban motorway

On a one-way street

Answer

On a one-way street

'Contraflow' means that the bus or cycle lane is going in the opposite direction to the other lanes in the road. Don't ride in or straddle these lanes.

Question 11.44

Mark one answer
What does this sign mean?

<ul>
<li>Bus station on the right</li>
<li>Contraflow bus lane</li>
<li>With-flow bus lane</li>
<li>Give way to buses</li>
</ul>

Answer

Contraflow bus lane

There will also be markings on the road surface to indicate the bus lane. Don't use this lane for parking or overtaking.

Question 11.45

Mark one answer
What does this sign mean?

<ul>
<li>With-flow bus and cycle lane</li>
<li>Contraflow bus and cycle lane</li>
<li>No buses and cycles allowed</li>
<li>No waiting for buses and cycles</li>
</ul>

Answer

With-flow bus and cycle lane

In this case buses and cycles may travel in this lane in the same direction as other traffic. There may be times shown on the sign to indicate when the lane is in use.

Mark one answer

What does a sign with a brown background show?

- Tourist directions
- Primary roads
- Motorway routes
- Minor routes

Answer

■ **Tourist directions**

Signs with a brown background give directions to places of interest. They will often be seen on the motorway directing you along the easiest route.

Question 11.47

Mark one answer

This sign means

- tourist attraction
- beware of trains
- level crossing
- beware of trams

Answer

■ **tourist attraction**

These signs indicate places of interest and are designed to guide you by the easiest route. If you are a tourist you're likely to be unfamiliar with the area, so these signs are particularly useful.

Question 11.48

Mark one answer

What are triangular signs for?

- To give warnings
- To give information
- To give orders
- To give directions

Answer

■ **To give warnings**

This type of sign will tell you about the road ahead and what to expect. Get into the habit of checking each sign that you pass. They will warn you of the hazards ahead.

DSA THEORY TEST for motorcyclists

Question 11.49

Mark one answer

What does this sign mean?

- Turn left ahead
- T-junction
- No through road
- Give way

Answer

T-junction

Look well down the road and check the road signs as you ride. You'll then be able to anticipate any junction hazards.

Question 11.50

Mark one answer

What does this sign mean?

- Multi-exit roundabout
- Risk of ice
- Six roads converge
- Place of historical interest

Answer

Risk of ice

It will take up to ten times longer to stop when it's icy. Consider this and ride carefully. Don't brake or steer harshly, as your tyres could lose their grip on the road.

Question 11.51

Mark one answer

What does this sign mean?

- Crossroads
- Level crossing with gate
- Level crossing without gate
- Ahead only

Answer

Crossroads

The priority through the junction is shown by the broader line. However, be aware of the danger when other traffic is crossing a major road.

Mark one answer

What does this sign mean?

▨ Ring road

▨ Mini-roundabout

▨ No vehicles

▨ Roundabout

Answer

▨ **Roundabout**

Prepare yourself for approaching hazards by checking signs as you ride.

Decide which exit you wish to take. Prepare to position your motorcycle correctly as you approach the roundabout.

Question 11.53

Mark four answers

Which FOUR of these would be indicated by a triangular road sign?

▨ Road narrows

▨ Ahead only

▨ Low bridge

▨ Minimum speed

▨ Children crossing

▨ T-junction

Answers

▨ **Road narrows**

▨ **Low bridge**

▨ **Children crossing**

▨ **T-junction**

Make use of the warning sign and be prepared for the hazard ahead.

Question 11.54

Mark one answer

What does this sign mean?

▨ Cyclists must dismount

▨ Cycles are not allowed

▨ Cycle route ahead

▨ Cycle in single file

Answer

▨ **Cycle route ahead**

Where there's a cycle route ahead, a sign will show a bicycle in a red warning triangle. Watch out for children on bicycles and cyclists rejoining the main road.

Question 11.55

Mark one answer

Which sign means that pedestrians may be walking along the road?

Answer

Be extra cautious, especially if there is a bend in the road and you're unable to see well ahead. When you pass, leave plenty of room. Consider that you might have to use the right hand side of the road, so look well ahead down the road, as well as in your mirrors, before you pull out.

Question 11.56

Mark one answer

Which of these signs warn you of a pedestrian crossing?

Answer

Look well ahead and check the pavements and surrounding areas for pedestrians. Keep an eye on those who are walking towards the crossing. Check your mirrors for traffic behind, in case you have to slow down or stop.

Mark one answer

What does this sign mean?

No footpath ahead

Pedestrians only ahead

Pedestrian crossing ahead

School crossing ahead

Answer

Pedestrian crossing ahead

There are many signs relating to pedestrians. Study *The Highway Code* and *Know Your Traffic Signs*. Some of the signs look similar but give different warnings. Make a mental note as you ride so that you're prepared for any potential hazard.

Mark one answer

What does this sign mean?

School crossing patrol

No pedestrians allowed

Pedestrian zone – no vehicles

Pedestrian crossing ahead

Answer

Pedestrian crossing ahead

Look well ahead and be ready to stop for any pedestrians crossing the road. Also check the pavements for anyone who looks like they might step off into the road.

Mark one answer

Which of these signs means there is a double bend ahead?

Answer

Triangular signs give you a warning of hazards ahead. They're there to give you time to adjust your speed and ride accordingly.

Question 11.60

Mark one answer

What does this sign mean?

- Wait at the barriers
- Wait at the crossroads
- Give way to trams
- Give way to farm vehicles

Question 11.61

Mark one answer

What does this sign mean?

- Humpback bridge
- Humps in the road
- Entrance to tunnel
- Soft verges

Answer

Give way to trams

Obey the 'GIVE WAY' signs. Trams are unable to steer around you or change their specific route.

Answer

Humps in the road

These have been put in place to slow the traffic down. They're usually found in residential areas. Slow down and ride at an appropriate speed.

Mark one answer

What does this sign mean?

Low bridge ahead

Tunnel ahead

Ancient monument ahead

Accident black spot ahead

Answer

Tunnel ahead

Be prepared to switch on your headlights, if required. Reduce your speed. Your eyes might need to adjust to the sudden darkness.

Mark one answer

What does this sign mean?

Two-way traffic straight ahead

Two-way traffic crossing a one-way street

Two-way traffic over a bridge

Two-way traffic crosses a two-way road

Answer

Two-way traffic crossing a one-way street

Be prepared for traffic approaching from junctions on either side of you.

Try to avoid unnecessary changing of lanes just before the junction.

DSA **THEORY TEST** for motorcyclists

Question 11.64

Mark one answer

Which sign means 'two-way traffic crosses a one-way road'?

Answer

Traffic could be joining the road you're in from either direction. Unless you need to turn, don't change lanes as you approach the junction.

Question 11.65

Mark one answer

Which of these signs means the end of a dual carriageway?

Answer

If you're travelling in the right-hand lane, prepare and move over into the left-hand lane as soon as it's safe to do so.

Mark one answer

What does this sign mean?

End of dual carriageway

Tall bridge

Road narrows

End of narrow bridge

Answer

End of dual carriageway

Don't leave moving into the left-hand lane until the last moment. Early planning will prevent you having to rely on other traffic letting you in.

Mark one answer

What does this sign mean?

Two-way traffic ahead across a one-way street

Traffic approaching you has priority

Two-way traffic straight ahead

Motorway contraflow system ahead

Answer

Two-way traffic straight ahead

This sign may be at the end of a dual carriageway or a one-way street. The sign is there to warn you of oncoming traffic.

Mark one answer

What does this sign mean?

Crosswinds

Road noise

Airport

Adverse camber

Answer

Crosswinds

Where weather conditions are often bad, signs will give you a warning. A sign with a picture of a windsock will indicate there may be strong crosswinds. This sign is often found on exposed roads.

DSA THEORY TEST for motorcyclist

Question 11.69

Mark one answer

What does this traffic sign mean?

Slippery road ahead

Tyres liable to punctures ahead

Danger ahead

Service area ahead

Answer

Danger ahead

A sign showing an exclamation mark (!) will alert you to the likelihood of danger ahead. Be ready for any situation that requires you to reduce your speed.

Question 11.70

Mark one answer

You are about to overtake when you see this sign. You should

overtake the other driver as quickly as possible

move to the right to get a better view

switch your headlights on before overtaking

hold back until you can see clearly ahead

Answer

hold back until you can see clearly ahead

You won't be able to see any hazards that might be out of sight in the dip.

Imagine there might be

- cyclists
- horse riders
- parked vehicles
- pedestrians.

There might also be oncoming traffic to deal with.

Question 11.71

Mark one answer
What does this sign mean?

- Level crossing with gate or barrier
- Gated road ahead
- Level crossing without gate or barrier
- Cattle grid ahead

Answer

Level crossing with gate or barrier

Some crossings have gates but no attendant or signals. You should

- stop
- look both ways
- listen and make sure that there is no tra[in] approaching.

If there is a telephone contact the signal operator to make sure that it's safe to cross.

Question 11.72

Mark one answer
What does this sign mean?

- No trams ahead
- Oncoming trams
- Trams crossing ahead
- Trams only

Answer

Trams crossing ahead

This is a warning sign. Watch out for trams. If you are not used to riding in a town where there are trams be especially careful at junctions. Watch out for road signs.

Question 11.73

Mark one answer
What does this sign mean?

- Adverse camber
- Steep hill downwards
- Uneven road
- Steep hill upwards

Answer

Steep hill downwards

This warning sign will give you an early indication. Prepare to alter your speed and gear. Looking at the sign from left to right, will show you whether it's up or downhill.

DSA THEORY TEST for motorcyclists

Question 11.74

Mark one answer

What does this sign mean?

- Quayside or river bank
- Steep hill downwards
- Slippery road
- Road liable to flooding

Answer

Quayside or river bank

Be aware that the road surface in this location is likely to be wet and slippery.

Question 11.75

Mark one answer

What does this sign mean?

- Uneven road surface
- Bridge over the road
- Road ahead ends
- Water across the road

Answer

Water across the road

This sign is found where a shallow stream crosses the road. Heavy rainfall could increase the flow of water. If the water looks too deep or the stream has swelled over a large distance, stop and find another route.

Question 11.76

Mark one answer

What does this sign mean?

- Humpback bridge
- Traffic calming hump
- Low bridge
- Uneven road

Answer

Humpback bridge

Slow right down. Riding over a humpback bridge too fast could cause your wheels to leave the road surface and result in a loss of control.

Mark one answer
What does this sign mean?

Turn left for parking area

No through road on the left

No entry for traffic turning left

Turn left for ferry terminal

Answer

No through road on the left

Signs are there to help you to ride and to help you to avoid making late decisions. If you intend to take a left turn, this sign shows you that you can't get through to another route.

Mark one answer
What does this sign mean?

T-junction

No through road

Telephone box ahead

Toilet ahead

Answer

No through road

You will not be able to find a through route to another road. Only use this road for access.

Mark one answer
Which sign means 'no through road'?

Answer

This sign is found at the entrance to the road

DSA THEORY TEST for motorcyclists

Question 11.80

Mark one answer

Which of the following signs informs you that you are coming to a No Through Road?

Answer

This sign is found at the entrance to the road.

Question 11.81

Mark one answer

What does this sign mean?

■ Direction to park and ride car park

■ No parking for buses or coaches

■ Directions to bus and coach park

■ Parking area for cars and coaches

Answer

■ **Direction to park and ride car park**

To ease the congestion in centres, some cities and towns provide a park and ride scheme. This allows you to park in a designated area and ride by bus into the centre. This is usually cheaper and easier than car parking in the centre.

Mark one answer

You are going through a tunnel and you see this sign. What does it mean?

▨ Direction to emergency pedestrian exit

▨ Beware of pedestrians, no footpath ahead

▨ No access for pedestrians

▨ Beware of pedestrians crossing ahead

Answer

▨ **Direction to emergency pedestrian exit**

If you find yourself having to evacuate a tunnel, do so as quickly as you can. Follow the signs, which will direct you to the nearest exit point. If there are a lot of people, don't panic but try to leave in a calm and orderly manner.

Mark one answer

Which is the sign for a ring road?

Answer

▨

Ring roads are designed to relieve congestion in towns and cities.

Mark one answer

What does this sign mean?

▨ Route for lorries

▨ Ring road

▨ Rest area

▨ Roundabout

Answer

▨ **Ring road**

Signs are also designed to give you advice. Ring road signs direct traffic around major towns and cities. Ring roads help the traffic to flow and ease congestion in town centres.

DSA THEORY TEST for motorcyclists

Question 11.85

Mark one answer
What does this sign mean?

- Hilly road
- Humps in road
- Holiday route
- Hospital route

Answer

Holiday route

In some areas where the volume of traffic increases during the summer months, signs show a route that diverts traffic away from town centres. This helps the traffic to flow, decreasing queues.

Question 11.86

Mark one answer
What does this sign mean?

- The right-hand lane ahead is narrow
- Right-hand lane for buses only
- Right-hand lane for turning right
- The right-hand lane is closed

Answer

The right-hand lane is closed

Temporary signs may tell you about roadworks or lane restrictions. Look well ahead. If you have to change lanes do so in good time.

Mark one answer

What does this sign mean?

- Change to the left lane
- Leave at the next exit
- Contraflow system
- One-way street

Answer

■ **Contraflow system**

If you use the right-hand lane, you'll be travelling with no permanent barrier betwe your motorcycle and the traffic coming towards you. Observe speed limits and keep good distance from the vehicle ahead.

Mark three answers

To avoid an accident when entering a contraflow system, you should

- reduce speed in good time
- switch lanes anytime to make progress
- choose an appropriate lane early
- keep the correct separation distance
- increase speed to pass through quickly
- follow other motorists closely to avoid long queues

Answers

■ **reduce speed in good time**

■ **choose an appropriate lane early**

■ **keep the correct separation distance**

In a contraflow system you will be travelling close to oncoming traffic and sometimes in narrow lanes. You should

- obey the temporary signs governing speed limits
- get into the correct lane in good time
- keep a safe separation distance from the vehicle ahead.

Question 11.89

Mark one answer

What does this sign mean?

- Leave motorway at next exit
- Lane for heavy and slow vehicles
- All lorries use the hard shoulder
- Rest area for lorries

Answer

Lane for heavy and slow vehicles

Where there's a long, steep, uphill gradient on a motorway there may be a crawler lane. This type of lane helps the traffic to flow by diverting the slower heavy vehicles into an extra lane on the left.

Question 11.90

Mark one answer

You see this traffic light ahead. Which light(s) will come on next?

- Red alone
- Red and amber together
- Green and amber together
- Green alone

Answer

Red alone

At junctions controlled by traffic lights you must stop behind the white line until the lights change to green. Don't

- move forward when the red and amber lights are showing together
- proceed when the light is green if your exit road is blocked.

If you're approaching traffic lights that are visible from a distance and the light has been green for some time it's likely to change. Try to anticipate this. Be ready to slow down and stop.

Mark one answer

You are approaching a red traffic light. The signal will change from red to

red and amber, then green

green, then amber

amber, then green

green and amber, then green

Answer

red and amber, then green

If you know which light is going to show next you can plan your approach according. This will prevent excessive braking or hesitation at the junction.

Mark one answer

A red traffic light means

you should stop unless turning left

stop, if you are able to brake safely

you must stop and wait behind the stop line

proceed with caution

Answer

you must stop and wait behind the stop line

Learn the sequence of traffic lights.

* RED means stop and wait behind the stop line.

* RED-AND-AMBER also means stop. Do go until the green light shows.

* GREEN means you may go if your way clear. Don't proceed if your exit road is blocked, and don't block the junction. Look out for pedestrians.

* AMBER means stop at the stop line. You may go if the amber light appears after you've crossed the stop line or you're so close to it that to pull up might cause an accident.

Question 11.93

Mark one answer

At traffic lights, amber on its own means

    prepare to go

    go if the way is clear

    go if no pedestrians are crossing

    stop at the stop line

Answer

    stop at the stop line

If the lights have been on green for a while they're likely to change as you approach. Anticipate this so that you're able to stop in time.

Question 11.94

Mark one answer

A red traffic light means

    you must stop behind the white stop line

    you may drive straight on if there is no other traffic

    you may turn left if it is safe to do so

    you must slow down and prepare to stop if traffic has started to cross

Answer

    you must stop behind the white stop line

The white line is positioned so that pedestrians have room to cross in front of waiting vehicles. If pedestrians are crossing make sure your brake is on.

Mark one answer

You are approaching traffic lights. Red and amber are showing. This means

▨ pass the lights if the road is clear

▨ there is a fault with the lights – take care

▨ wait for the green light before you pass the lights

▨ the lights are about to change to red

Answer

▨ **wait for the green light before you pass the lights**

Other traffic might still be clearing the junction. Don't take risks.

Mark one answer

You are at a junction controlled by traffic lights. When should you NOT proceed at green?

▨ When pedestrians are waiting to cross

▨ When your exit from the junction is blocked

▨ When you think the lights may be about to change

▨ When you intend to turn right

Answer

▨ **When your exit from the junction is blocked**

As you approach the lights look into the ro. you wish to take. Only proceed if your exit road is clear. If the road is blocked hold bac even if you have to wait for the next green signal.

DSA THEORY TEST for motorcyclis•

Question 11.97

Mark one answer

You are in the left-hand lane at traffic lights. You are waiting to turn left. At which of these traffic lights must you NOT move on?

Answer

At some junctions there may be a separate signal for each lane. These are called 'filter' lights. They're designed to help traffic flow at major junctions. Make sure that you're in the correct lane, and proceed if the green light shows.

Question 11.98

Mark one answer

What does this sign mean?

- [ ] Traffic lights out of order
- [ ] Amber signal out of order
- [ ] Temporary traffic lights ahead
- [ ] New traffic lights ahead

Answer

Traffic lights out of order

Where traffic lights are out of order you might see this sign. Proceed with caution as nobody has priority at the junction.

Mark one answer

You see this sign at a crossroads. You should

maintain the same speed

carry on with great care

find another route

telephone the police

Answer

carry on with great care

Only do so if the road is clear. Treat the road if it was an unmarked junction, that is, no one has priority.

Mark one answer

When traffic lights are out of order, who has priority?

Traffic going straight on

Traffic turning right

Nobody

Traffic turning left

Answer

Nobody

Treat the junction as an unmarked crossroads. Deal with the situation with caution.

Mark three answers

These flashing red lights mean STOP. In which THREE of the following places could you find them?

Pelican crossings

Lifting bridges

Zebra crossings

Level crossings

Motorway exits

Fire stations

Answers

Lifting bridges

Level crossings

Fire stations

Don't take risks by trying to beat the lights, even if it's clear. You must stop.

DSA THEORY TEST for motorcyclist

Question 11.102

Mark one answer

What do these zigzag lines at pedestrian crossings mean?

- No parking at any time
- Parking allowed only for a short time
- Slow down to 20 mph
- Sounding horns is not allowed

Answer

No parking at any time

The approach to hazards may be marked with signs on the road surface. The approach to a pedestrian crossing is marked with zigzag lines.

Don't

- park on them
- overtake the leading vehicle when approaching the crossing.

Parking here will block the view for pedestrians and the approaching traffic.

Question 11.103

Mark one answer

The white line along the side of the road

- shows the edge of the carriageway
- shows the approach to a hazard
- means no parking
- means no overtaking

Answer

shows the edge of the carriageway

This is found at the edge of the road other than at junctions. It can be especially useful when visibility is restricted.

Mark one answer

The white line painted in the centre of the road means

Answer

■ **do not cross the line unless the road ahead is clear**

A long white line with short gaps is a warning line, so if you wish to overtake or need to turn, consider the risks.

■ the area is hazardous and you must not overtake

■ you should give priority to oncoming vehicles

■ do not cross the line unless the road ahead is clear

■ the area is a national speed limit zone

Mark one answer

When may you cross a double solid white line in the middle of the road?

Answer

■ **To pass a road maintenance vehicle travelling at 10 mph or less**

Only overtake such a vehicle if you're sure that you can complete the manoeuvre safely. Keep well back before you overtake so that you have a clear view of the road. Double solid white lines indicate that there are hazards, such as bends in the road or junctions, so be extra cautious.

■ To pass traffic that is queuing back at a junction

■ To pass a car signalling to turn left ahead

■ To pass a road maintenance vehicle travelling at 10 mph or less

■ To pass a vehicle that is towing a trailer

Question 11.106

Mark one answer

A white line like this along the centre of the road is a

- bus lane marking
- hazard warning
- 'give way' marking
- lane marking

Answer

☐ **hazard warning**

Make a note of hazard lines as you ride. Look well ahead and around so that you're prepared for any potential dangers.

Question 11.107

Mark one answer

You see this white arrow on the road ahead. It means

- entrance on the left
- all vehicles turn left
- keep left of the hatched markings
- road bending to the left

Answer

☐ **keep left of the hatched markings**

Don't attempt to overtake here, there might be unseen hazards over the brow of the hill; keep to the left.

Mark one answer
What does this road marking mean?

Do not cross the line

No stopping allowed

You are approaching a hazard

No overtaking allowed

Answer

You are approaching a hazard

Road markings will warn you of a hazard
ahead. A single broken line, with long
markings and short gaps, along the centre of
the road is a hazard warning line. Don't cross
it unless you can see that the road is clear
WELL ahead.

Mark one answer
This marking appears on the road just
before a

no entry sign

give way sign

stop sign

no through road sign

Answer

give way sign

You must give way to the traffic on the main
road. This road marking might not be used at
junctions where there is relatively little
traffic. The give way rules still apply.

Question 11.110

Mark one answer
Where would you see this road marking?

■ At traffic lights

■ On road humps

■ Near a level crossing

■ At a box junction

Answer

■ **On road humps**

Due to the dark colour of the road, changes in surface aren't easily seen. White triangles painted on the road surface give you an indication of where there are road humps.

Question 11.111

Mark one answer
Which is a hazard warning line?

Answer

Look out for places where the single broken line on the road surface gets longer. This will mean there's a hazard ahead.

Mark one answer

At this junction there is a stop sign with a solid white line on the road surface. Why is there a stop sign here?

Speed on the major road is de-restricted

It is a busy junction

Visibility along the major road is restricted

There are hazard warning lines in the centre of the road

Answer

Visibility along the major road is restricted

If your view is restricted at a road junction you must stop. There may also be a stop sign Don't emerge until you're sure there's no traffic approaching.

IF YOU DON'T KNOW, DON'T GO.

Mark one answer

You see this line across the road at the entrance to a roundabout. What does it mean?

Give way to traffic from the right

Traffic from the left has right of way

You have right of way

Stop at the line

Answer

Give way to traffic from the right

Slow down as you approach, checking the traffic as you do so. If you need to stop and give way, stay behind the broken line until it is safe to emerge onto the roundabout.

Question 11.114

Mark one answer

Where would you find this road marking?

- At a railway crossing
- At a junction
- On a motorway
- On a pedestrian crossing

Answer

■ **At a junction**

This marking indicates the direction in which the traffic should flow.

Question 11.115

Mark one answer

How will a police officer in a patrol vehicle normally get you to stop?

- Flash the headlights, indicate left and point to the left
- Wait until you stop, then approach you
- Use the siren, overtake, cut in front and stop
- Pull alongside you, use the siren and wave you to stop

Answer

■ **Flash the headlights, indicate left and point to the left**

You must obey signals given by the police. If a police officer in a patrol vehicle wants you to stop he or she will indicate this without causing danger to you or other traffic.

Question 11.116

Mark one answer

There is a police car following you. The police officer flashes the headlights and points to the left. What should you do?

- Turn at the next left
- Pull up on the left
- Stop immediately
- Move over to the left

Answer

■ **Pull up on the left**

You must pull up on the left, as soon as it's safe to do so, and switch off your engine.

Question 11.117

Mark one answer

You approach a junction. The traffic lights are not working. A police officer gives this signal. You should

	turn left only
	turn right only
	stop level with the officer's arm
	stop at the stop line

Answer

| | **stop at the stop line** |

If a police officer or traffic warden is directing traffic you must obey them. They will use the arm signals shown in *The Highway Code*. Learn what these mean and act accordingly.

Question 11.118

Mark one answer

The driver of the car in front is giving this arm signal. What does it mean?

	The driver is slowing down
	The driver intends to turn right
	The driver wishes to overtake
	The driver intends to turn left

Answer

| | **The driver intends to turn left** |

There might be an occasion where another driver uses an arm signal. This may be because the vehicle's indicators are obscured by other traffic. In order for such signals to be effective all drivers should know the meaning of them.

Be aware that the 'left turn' signal might look similar to the 'slowing down' signal

DSA THEORY TEST for motorcyclist

Question 11.119

Mark one answer

The driver of this car is giving an arm signal. What is he about to do?

Turn to the right

Turn to the left

Go straight ahead

Let pedestrians cross

Answer

Turn to the left

For arm signals to be effective all road users should know their meaning.

Question 11.120

Mark one answer

You are signalling to turn right in busy traffic. How would you confirm your intention safely?

Sound the horn

Give an arm signal

Flash your headlights

Position over the centre line

Answer

Give an arm signal

In some situations you may feel your indicators cannot be seen by other road users. If you feel you need to make your intention more clearly seen, give the arm signal shown in *The Highway Code*.

Question 11.121

Mark one answer

How should you give an arm signal to turn left?

Answer

Arm signals are very effective during daylight, especially when you're wearing bright clothing.

Practise giving arm signals when you're learning. You need to be able to keep full control of your motorcycle with one hand off the handlebars.

Mark one answer

Your indicators are difficult to see due to bright sunshine. When using them you should

- ▨ also give an arm signal
- ▨ sound your horn
- ▨ flash your headlamp
- ▨ keep both hands on the handlebars

Answer

▨ **also give an arm signal**

Arm signals are effective when you aren't sure that your indicators can be seen by other road users. Make sure that your signal is decisive, and return your hand to the handlebars before you turn.

Mark one answer

You are giving an arm signal ready to turn left. Why should you NOT continue with the arm signal while you turn?

- ▨ Because you might hit a pedestrian on the corner
- ▨ Because you will have less steering control
- ▨ Because you will need to keep the clutch applied
- ▨ Because other motorists will think that you are stopping on the corner

Answer

▨ **Because you will have less steering control**

Don't maintain an arm signal when turning. You should have full control of your motorcycle at all times.

Mark one answer

You want to turn right at a junction but you think that your indicators cannot be seen clearly. What should you do?

- ▨ Get out and check if your indicators can be seen
- ▨ Stay in the left-hand lane
- ▨ Keep well over to the right
- ▨ Give an arm signal as well as an indicator signal

Answer

▨ **Give an arm signal as well as an indicator signal**

If you think that your indicators can't be seen clearly due to other vehicles obscuring them, make sure that your intention is clear by using an arm signal too.

Question 11.125

Mark one answer

When may you sound the horn on your motorcycle?

- To give you right of way
- To attract a friend's attention
- To warn others of your presence
- To make slower drivers move over

Answer

To warn others of your presence

Don't use the horn aggressively. You must not sound it

- between 11.30 pm and 7 am
- when your motorcycle is stationary, unless a moving vehicle poses a danger.

Question 11.126

Mark one answer

You must not use your horn when your motorcycle is stationary

- unless a moving vehicle may cause you danger
- at any time whatsoever
- unless it is used only briefly
- except for signalling that you have just arrived

Answer

unless a moving vehicle may cause you danger

Do this only if you think that there is a risk of an accident. Don't use as for attracting the attention of others for social reasons.

Question 11.127

Mark one answer

When motorists flash their headlights at you it means

- that there is a radar speed trap ahead
- that they are giving way to you
- that they are warning you of their presence
- that there is something wrong with your motorcycle

Answer

that they are warning you of their presence

If other drivers flash their headlights this isn't a signal to show priority. The flashing of headlights has the same meaning as sounding the horn – it's a warning of their presence.

Mark one answer

Why should you make sure that you have cancelled your indicators after turning?

▨ To avoid flattening the battery

▨ To avoid misleading other road users

▨ To avoid dazzling other road users

▨ To avoid damage to the indicator relay

Answer

▨ **To avoid misleading other road users**

If you haven't taken a sharp turn your indicators might not turn off automatically. Be aware of this if you've used them for slight deviations, such as passing parked vehicles.

Mark one answer

Where would you see these road markings?

▨ At a level crossing

▨ On a motorway slip road

▨ At a pedestrian crossing

▨ On a single-track road

Answer

▨ **On a motorway slip road**

You must not enter into the area marked except in an emergency.

Mark one answer

When may you NOT overtake on the left?

▨ On a free-flowing motorway or dual carriageway

▨ When the traffic is moving slowly in queues

▨ On a one-way street

▨ When the car in front is signalling to turn right

Answer

▨ **On a free-flowing motorway or dual carriageway**

You may only overtake on the left

• when traffic is moving slowly in queues

• when a vehicle ahead is positioned to turn right and there's room to pass on the left

• in a one-way street.

Don't overtake on the left if the traffic on a dual carriageway is flowing freely. Other road users won't anticipate your action.

Question 11.131

Mark one answer

You are riding on a motorway. There is a slow-moving vehicle ahead. On the back you see this sign. You should

- pass on the right
- pass on the left
- leave at the next exit
- drive no further

Answer

- **pass on the left**

You'll have to change lanes in order to pass the vehicle. Use your mirror and signal. If it's safe to do so, move over into the lane on your left. Look well down the road so that you can spot such hazards early, leaving you time to complete the manoeuvre safely.

Question 11.132

Mark one answer

What does this motorway sign mean?

- Change to the lane on your left
- Leave the motorway at the next exit
- Change to the opposite carriageway
- Pull up on the hard shoulder

Answer

- **Change to the lane on your left**

On the motorway, signs might show temporary warnings. This allows for different traffic or weather conditions and might indicate

- lane closures
- speed limits
- weather warnings.

Mark one answer

What does this motorway sign mean?

⬜ Temporary minimum speed 50 mph

⬜ No services for 50 miles

⬜ Obstruction 50 metres (164 feet) ahead

⬜ Temporary maximum speed 50 mph

Answer

⬜ **Temporary maximum speed 50 mph**

Look out for signs above your lane or on the central reserve. These will give you important information or warnings about the road ahead.

Due to the high speeds of motorway traffic these signs may light up some distance from any hazard. Don't ignore the signs just because the road looks clear to you.

Mark one answer

What does this sign mean?

⬜ Through traffic to use left lane

⬜ Right-hand lane T-junction only

⬜ Right-hand lane closed ahead

⬜ 11 tonne weight limit

Answer

⬜ **Right-hand lane closed ahead**

Move over as soon as you see the sign and it safe to do so. Don't stay in the lane, which is closed ahead, until the last moment to beat a queue of traffic.

DSA THEORY TEST for motorcyclists

Question 11.135

Mark one answer

On a motorway this sign means

☐ move over onto the hard shoulder

☐ overtaking on the left only

☐ leave the motorway at the next exit

☐ move to the lane on your left

Answer

☐ **move to the lane on your left**

On the motorway, signs might show temporary warnings. This allows for different traffic or weather conditions and might indicate

• lane closures

• speed limits

• weather warnings.

Question 11.136

Mark one answer

What does '25' mean on this motorway sign?

☐ The distance to the nearest town

☐ The route number of the road

☐ The number of the next junction

☐ The speed limit on the slip road

Answer

☐ **The number of the next junction**

Before you set out on your journey use a road map to plan your route.

You should give yourself enough time to get into the correct lane for the exit that you wish to take. Uncertainty at road junctions can lead to danger.

Question 11.137

Mark one answer

You are on a motorway. Red flashing lights appear above your lane only. What should you do?

- Continue in that lane and await further information
- Go no further in that lane
- Pull onto the hard shoulder
- Stop and wait for an instruction to proceed

Answer

Go no further in that lane

Flashing red lights above your lane show that your lane is closed. You should move into a clear lane in plenty of time.

Question 11.138

Mark one answer

The right-hand lane of a three-lane motorway is

- for lorries only
- an overtaking lane
- the right-turn lane
- an acceleration lane

Answer

an overtaking lane

Motorways today can become very busy. If a vehicle in the right-hand lane is preventing traffic to the rear from overtaking, or is travelling at a slower speed than those on the nearside, bunching can occur. This means that drivers will begin to travel too close to the vehicle in front of them. If you aren't overtaking, use the left-hand lane.

Question 11.139

Mark one answer

Where can you find reflective amber studs on a motorway?

- Separating the slip road from the motorway
- On the left-hand edge of the road
- On the right-hand edge of the road
- Separating the lanes

Answer

On the right-hand edge of the road

At night or in poor visibility reflective studs on the road will help you to judge your position on the carriageway.

Question 11.140

Mark one answer

Where on a motorway would you find green reflective studs?

- Separating driving lanes
- Between the hard shoulder and the carriageway
- At slip road entrances and exits
- Between the carriageway and the central reservation

Answer

At slip road entrances and exits

Knowing the colours of the reflective studs on the road will help you in foggy conditions or when visibility is poor.

Question 11.141

Mark one answer

You are travelling along a motorway. You see this sign. You should

- leave the motorway at the next exit
- turn left immediately
- change lane
- move onto the hard shoulder

Answer

leave the motorway at the next exit

You'll see this sign if the motorway is closed ahead. When you see it prepare to get into the nearside lane so that you can take the exit safely. Don't leave it to the last moment.

Mark one answer

You see these signs overhead on the motorway. They mean

- [ ] leave the motorway at the next exit
- [ ] all vehicles use the hard shoulder
- [ ] sharp bend to the left ahead
- [ ] stop, all lanes ahead closed

Answer

- [ ] **leave the motorway at the next exit**

There has been an incident ahead and the motorway is closed. You must obey the sign. Make sure that you prepare to leave as soon as you see them. Don't leave it until the last moment by cutting across other traffic.

Mark one answer

Which of these signs means that the national speed limit applies?

Answer

You should know the speed limit for the road that you're travelling on and the vehicle that you're driving. Study your copy of *The Highway Code*, where the limits are clearly shown.

Mark one answer

What is the maximum speed on a single carriageway road?

- [ ] 50 mph
- [ ] 60 mph
- [ ] 40 mph
- [ ] 70 mph

Answer

- [ ] **60 mph**

If you're travelling on a dual carriageway that becomes a single carriageway road, cut your speed gradually so that you aren't exceeding the limit as you enter it. There might not be a sign to remind you of the limit, so learn the speed limits.

Question 11.145

Mark one answer

What does this sign mean?

- Motorcycles only
- No cars
- Cars only
- No motorcycles

Answer

No motorcycles

You must comply with all traffic signs and be especially aware of those signs which apply specifically to the type of vehicle you are using.

Question 11.146

Mark one answer

You are on a motorway. You see this sign on a lorry that has stopped in the right-hand lane. You should

- move into the right-hand lane
- stop behind the flashing lights
- pass the lorry on the left
- leave the motorway at the next exit

Answer

pass the lorry on the left

Sometimes it is possible to carry out work on the motorway without closing the lanes. In such cases, signs are mounted on the back of lorries to warn other road users of road works ahead.

Mark one answer

This sign is of particular importance to motorcyclists. It means

- side winds
- airport
- slippery road
- service area

Answer

■ **side winds**

Strong crosswinds can suddenly blow you off course. Keep your speed down when it is very windy, especially on exposed roads.

Mark one answer

What does this sign mean?

- End of motorway
- End of restriction
- Lane ends ahead
- Free recovery ends

Answer

■ **End of restriction**

At the end of the restriction you will see this sign without any flashing lights.

Question 11.149

Mark one answer

This sign is advising you to

- follow the route diversion
- follow the signs to the picnic area
- give way to pedestrians
- give way to cyclists

Answer

- **follow the route diversion**

These symbols guide drivers on diversion routes that may have been imposed by a road closure or an accident on a motorway or other main road.

Question 11.150

Mark one answer

Why would this temporary speed limit sign be shown?

- To warn of the end of the motorway
- To warn you of a low bridge
- To warn you of a junction ahead
- To warn of road works ahead

Answer

- **To warn of road works ahead**

To lessen the chance of accidents happening, most major roadworks have reduced speed limits imposed. You should always comply with them.

Mark one answer

Which one of these signs are you allowed to ride past on a solo motorcycle?

Answer

Most regulatory signs are circular; a red circle gives a prohibitory instruction.

Mark one answer

Which of these signals should you give when slowing or stopping your motorcycle?

Answer

Arm signals can be given to reinforce your flashing indicators, especially if the indicator signal could cause confusion, e.g., if you intend to pull up close to a side road.

SECTION 12 DOCUMENTS

This section looks at the documents needed for riders
and their motorcycles.

The questions will ask you about

- **Licences**

  you must know what the law requires.

- **Insurance**

  you must have the cover you need to ride.

- **MOT test certificate**

  you should be aware of the safety checks your
  motorcycle must undergo to gain an MOT certificate.

Question 12.1

Mark one answer

Your driving licence must be signed by

- a police officer
- a driving instructor
- your next of kin
- yourself

Answer

☐ **yourself**

Do this when you apply for your licence.

Question 12.2

Mark four answers

You have passed CBT (Compulsory Basic Training). You want a Direct Access test. You must

- be aged 21 or over
- not exceed 60 mph
- have an approved instructor with you
- remain in radio contact while learning
- only learn in daylight hours
- wear fluorescent or reflective clothing

Answers

☐ **be aged 21 or over**
☐ **have an approved instructor with you**
☐ **remain in radio contact while learning**
☐ **wear fluorescent or reflective clothing**

If you wish to learn to ride a motorcycle via the direct access route you must be at least 21 years old. When practising on the road you must

- have L plates fitted (D plates in Wales)
- be accompanied by an approved instructor in radio contact
- wear fluorescent or reflective safety clothing.

Question 12.3

Mark one answer

You want a licence to ride a large motorcycle via direct access. You will

- not require L plates if you have passed a car test
- require L plates only when learning on your own machine
- require L plates while learning with a qualified instructor
- not require L plates if you have passed a moped test

Answer

☐ **require L plates while learning with a qualified instructor**

While training through the direct access scheme you must be accompanied by an instructor on another motorcycle and in radio contact. You will have to display L plates on your motorcycle and follow all normal learner restrictions.

Question 12.4

Mark one answer

You are a learner motorcyclist. The law states that you can carry a passenger when

- your motorcycle is no larger than 125cc
- your pillion passenger is a full licence-holder
- you have passed your test for a full licence
- you have had three years' experience of riding

Answer

- **you have passed your test for a full licence**

When you're a learner motorcyclist you must comply with certain legal restrictions. The law states that you must

- display L plates (D plates in Wales) to the front and rear on your motorcycle
- not carry pillion passengers
- not use the motorway.

Question 12.5

Mark three answers

What should you bring with you when taking your motorcycle test?

- A service record book
- An insurance certificate
- A signed driving licence
- An MOT certificate
- A CBT (Compulsory Basic Training) certificate
- Signed photo identity

Answers

- **A signed driving licence**
- **A CBT (Compulsory Basic Training) certificate**
- **Signed photo identity**

When you attend a motorcycle test your examiner will ask to see

- your driving licence
- your CBT certificate (except in Northern Ireland).
- signed photo ID

Question 12.6

Mark one answer

Before taking a motorcycle test you need

- a full moped licence
- a full car licence
- a CBT (Compulsory Basic Training) certificate
- 12 months riding experience

Answer

- **a CBT (Compulsory Basic Training) certificate**

You can find out about a CBT course by asking your motorcycle dealer or by telephoning 0115 901 2595.

In Northern Ireland the CBT scheme doesn't operate, so all reference to CBT isn't applicable.

Question 12.7

Mark one answer

Compulsory Basic Training (CBT) can only be carried out by

- any ADI (Approved Driving Instructor)
- any road safety officer
- any DSA (Driving Standards Agency) approved training body
- any motorcycle main dealer

Answer

- **any DSA (Driving Standards Agency) approved training body**

DSA approves bodies to provide training in a safe environment. Frequent checks are made to ensure a high standard of instruction. Taking a CBT course will provide you with the right start to your motorcycling life.

Question 12.8

Mark one answer

After passing your motorcycle test you must exchange the pass certificate for a full motorcycle licence within

- six months
- one year
- two years
- five years

Answer

- **two years**

When you pass your practical motorcycle test you'll be issued with a pass certificate (form D.10 – DL8 in Northern Ireland). You must exchange the certificate for a full licence within two years of passing your test. If you don't

- the certificate will lapse
- you'll have to retake your test if you wish to resume full motorcycle licence entitlement.

Question 12.9

Mark one answer

Vehicle excise duty is often called 'Road Tax' or 'The Tax Disc'. You must

- keep it with your registration document
- display it clearly on your motorcycle
- keep it concealed safely in your motorcycle
- carry it on you at all times

Answer

- **display it clearly on your motorcycle**

It should be clearly displayed. It must be current, and you can't transfer the disc to another vehicle.

Question 12.10

Mark two answers

For which TWO of these must you show your motorcycle insurance certificate?

- When you are taking your motorcycle test
- When buying or selling a motorcycle
- When a police officer asks you for it
- When you are taxing your motorcycle
- When having an MOT inspection

Answers

- **When a police officer asks you for it**
- **When you are taxing your motorcycle**

You don't have to carry it with you at all times. However, it must be valid and available to present at a police station (within 7 days) if requested.

Question 12.11

Mark one answer

A police officer asks to see your documents. You do not have them with you. You may produce them at a police station within

- five days
- seven days
- 14 days
- 21 days

Answer

- **seven days**

You don't have to carry your documents with you. If a police officer asks to see them and you don't have them with you, you may produce them at a police station within seven days (five days in Northern Ireland).

Question 12.12

Mark one answer

Before riding anyone else's motorcycle you should make sure that

- the motorcycle owner has third party insurance cover
- your own motorcycle has insurance cover
- the motorcycle is insured for your use
- the owner has the insurance documents with them

Answer

- **the motorcycle is insured for your use**

If you borrow a motorcycle you must make sure that you're insured. Find out yourself. Don't take anyone else's word for it.

Question 12.13

Mark one answer

What is the legal minimum insurance cover you must have to ride on public roads?

- Third party, fire and theft
- Fully comprehensive
- Third party only
- Personal injury cover

Answer

Third party only

The minimum insurance requirement by law is third party cover. This covers others involved in an accident but not damage to your motorcycle. Basic third party insurance won't cover theft or fire damage. Check with your insurance company for advice on the best cover for you. Make sure that you read the policy carefully.

Question 12.14

Mark one answer

Motorcycles must FIRST have an MOT test certificate when they are

- one year old
- three years old
- five years old
- seven years old

Answer

three years old

The motorcycle you ride must be in good condition and roadworthy. If it's over three years old it must have a valid MOT test certificate.

In Northern Ireland a motorcycle first needs an MOT test certificate when it's four years old.

Question 12.15

Mark one answer

An MOT certificate is normally valid for

- three years after the date it was issued
- 10,000 miles
- one year after the date it was issued
- 30,000 miles

Answer

one year after the date it was issued

Make a note of the date that your motorcycle is due for an MOT. Some garages remind you, but not all of them.

Mark one answer

Your motorcycle needs a current MOT certificate. You do not have one. Until you do have one you will not be able to renew your

▨ driving licence

▨ vehicle insurance

▨ road tax disc

▨ vehicle registration document

Answer

▨ **road tax disc**

You'll have to produce your MOT certificate when you renew your road tax disc (road fund licence).

Question 12.17

Mark two answers

Which TWO of these are NOT required to have an MOT certificate?

▨ Motor cycle

▨ Small trailer

▨ Ambulance

▨ Caravan

Answers

▨ **Small trailer**

▨ **Caravan**

Despite not needing an MOT certificate, you should ensure that your trailer is in good order and properly serviced. Tyres, wheel nuts, lights and indicators should be checked regularly.

Question 12.18

Mark three answers

Which THREE of the following do you need before you can ride legally?

▨ A valid signed driving licence

▨ A valid tax disc displayed on your motorcycle

▨ Proof of your identity

▨ Proper insurance cover

▨ Breakdown cover

▨ A motorcycle handbook

Answers

▨ **A valid signed driving licence**

▨ **A valid tax disc displayed on your motorcycle**

▨ **Proper insurance cover**

Make sure that your motorcycle is not only safe but legal.

Question 12.19

Mark one answer

CBT (Compulsory Basic Training) completion certificates (DL196) issued on or after 01 July 1996 are valid for

▨ two years

▨ three years

▨ five years

▨ indefinitely

Answer

▨ **three years**

In order to complete the CBT course you'll have to demonstrate that you can ride confidently and safely in a variety of road and traffic conditions. Your certificate will enable you to apply for your tests. If you don't pass your tests within its three-year life you'll have to complete the CBT course again.

Question 12.20

Mark one answer

When you buy a motorcycle you will need a vehicle registration document from

▨ any MOT testing station

▨ the person selling the motorcycle

▨ your local council offices

▨ your local trading standards officer

Answer

▨ **the person selling the motorcycle**

You must fill in your details and send it to the Driver and Vehicle Licensing Agency (DVLA) at the address given on the document.

Mark three answers

Which THREE pieces of information are found on a vehicle registration document?

- Registered keeper
- Make of the motorcycle
- Service history details
- Date of the MOT
- Type of insurance cover
- Engine size

Answers

- **Registered keeper**
- **Make of the vehicle**
- **Engine size**

Every motorcycle used on the road has a registration document. This is issued by the Driver Vehicle Licensing Agency (DVLA) or the Driver and Vehicle Licensing Northern Ireland (DVLNI) and it keeps a record of changes of ownership. The document states

- date of first registration
- registration number
- previous keeper
- registered keeper
- make of motorcycle
- engine size and frame number
- year of manufacture
- colour.

Mark three answers

You have a duty to contact the licensing authority when

- you go abroad on holiday
- you change your motorcycle
- you change your name
- your job status is changed
- your permanent address changes
- your job involves travelling abroad

Answers

- **you change your motorcycle**
- **you change your name**
- **your permanent address changes**

The licensing authority need to keep their records up to date. You will receive a reminder when your road tax is due and they will need your current address for this purpose. Every motorcycle in the country is registered, so it's possible to trace its history.

DOCUMENTS

Question 12.23

Mark three answers

You must notify the licensing authority when

- your health affects your riding
- your eyesight does not meet a set standard
- you intend lending your motorcycle
- your motorcycle requires an MOT certificate
- you change your motorcycle

Answers

- **your health affects your riding**
- **your eyesight does not meet a set standard**
- **you change your motorcycle**

The Driver and Vehicle Licensing Agency (DVLA) hold the records of all motorcycles and riders in Great Britain. They need to know of any change in circumstances so that they can keep their records up to date. Your health might affect your ability to ride safely. This should not be underestimated, as you and others on the road could be at risk.

Question 12.24

Mark one answer

You have just bought a secondhand motorcycle. When should you tell the licensing authority of change of ownership?

- Immediately
- After 28 days
- When an MOT is due
- Only when you insure it

Answer

- **Immediately**

As soon as you can, fill out the registration document of the motorcycle and send it off. The requirements will be written on the document. It is an offence not to notify the licensing agency.

Question 12.25

Mark two answers

Your motorcycle is insured third party only. This covers

- damage to your motorcycle
- damage to other vehicles
- injury to yourself
- injury to others
- all damage and injury

Answers

- **damage to other vehicles**
- **injury to others**

This type of insurance cover is usually cheaper than fully comprehensive. However, it does not cover any damage to your own motorcycle or property. It is solely to cover damage and/or injury to others.

DSA THEORY TEST **for motorcyclists**

287

Mark three answers

You hold a provisional motorcycle licence. This means you must NOT

- ☐ exceed 30mph
- ☐ ride on a motorway
- ☐ ride after dark
- ☐ carry a pillion passenger
- ☐ ride without 'L' plates displayed

Answers

- ☐ ride on a motorway
- ☐ carry a pillion passenger
- ☐ ride without 'L' plates displayed

Provisional entitlement means that many restrictions apply to your use of motorcycles.

Most of the requirements are there to protect you and other road users. Make sure you are well aware of the requirements before you ride your motorcycle on the road.

Mark three answers

Which of the following information is found on your motorcycle registration document?

- ☐ Make and model
- ☐ Service history record
- ☐ Ignition key security number
- ☐ Engine size and number
- ☐ Purchase price
- ☐ Year of first registration

Answers

- ☐ Make and model
- ☐ Engine size and number
- ☐ Year of first registration

The vehicle registration document contains details of your motorcycle's make and model

- when it was first registered
- engine size and number

If you buy a new motorcycle the dealer will register your motorcycle with the licensing authority who will send the registration document to you.

Mark one answer

A theory test pass certificate will not be valid after

- ☐ 6 months
- ☐ 1year
- ☐ 18 months
- ☐ 2 years

Answer

- ☐ 2 years

A theory test pass certificate is valid for two years. If after two years you have not passed your practical test you will have to retake your theory test again.

Question 12.29

Mark one answer

A theory test pass certificate is valid for

- two years
- three years
- four years
- five years

Answer

two years

Your pass certificate is valid for only two years. If you don't pass your practical test for that category of vehicle within two years you will have to retake your theory test.

Question 12.30

Mark one answer

Your motorcycle insurance policy has an excess of £100. What does this mean?

- The insurance company will pay the first £100 of any claim
- You will be paid £100 if you do not have an accident
- Your motorcycle is insured for a value of £100 if it is stolen
- You will have to pay the first £100 of any claim

Answer

You will have to pay the first £100 of any claim

You will have to pay the first £100 pounds of any claim. It is a method that insurance companies use to keep annual premiums down. It is usually the case where the higher the excess you choose to pay, then the lower the annual premium you will be charged.

Question 12.31

Mark two answers

You have just passed your motorcycle test. Within two years you get six penalty points on your licence. You will have to

- retake only your theory test
- retake your theory and practical tests
- retake only your practical test
- re-apply for your full licence immediately
- re-apply for your provisional licence

Answers

retake your theory and practical tests

re-apply for your provisional licence

Your licence will be revoked if the number of penalty points on your licence reaches six or more, as a result of offences you commit before the two years are over. This includes offences you committed before you passed your test.

You may only ride as a learner until you pass both the theory and practical tests again.

Mark one answer

A cover note is a document issued before you receive your

- driving licence
- insurance certificate
- registration document
- MOT certificate

Answer

insurance certificate

Sometimes an insurance company will issue temporary insurance certificate called a cover note. It gives you the same insurance cover your certificate, but will only last for a limited period, usually one month.

Question 12.33

Mark one answer

When you apply to renew your motorcycle excise licence (tax disc) you must produce

- a valid insurance certificate
- the old tax disc
- the motorcycle handbook
- a valid driving licence

Answer

a valid insurance certificate

Tax discs can be renewed at most post offices, your nearest vehicle registration offi or by post to the licensing authority. Make sure you take all the relevant documents wit your application.

Question 12.34

Mark one answer

What is the legal minimum insurance cover you must have to ride on public roads?

- Fire and theft
- Theft only
- Third party
- Fire only

Answer

Third party

Third party insurance is the minimum cover you must have to be able to ride on the public roads. This means it only covers damage and/or injury that you may cause to other persons or property. It does not cover any damage to your motorcycle or property.

Question 12.35

Mark one answer

A full category A1 licence will allow you to ride a motorcycle up to

- 125 cc
- 250 cc
- 350 cc
- 425 cc

Answer

125 cc

When you pass your test on a motorcycle between 75 cc and 125 cc you will be issued with a full light motorcycle licence of category A1. You will then be allowed to rid any motorcycle up to 125 cc, and with a power output of 11 Kw (14.6bhp).

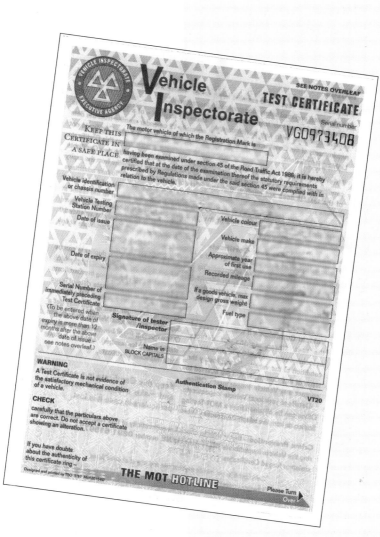

Don't lose it!

So you're about to buy your scooter or motor-cycle - or maybe you've already got it.
But beware, your pride and joy will be just as attractive to thieves as it is to you.
Motorcycles are an easy target for thieves, and all types of machines are at risk.

However, help is at hand.
By taking simple precautions, you can dramatically reduce the chances of theft.
A leaflet, "Don't give them an easy ride" explaining all you need to know about security is available from most motorcycle dealers or your local Crime Prevention Officer. Get a copy now before it's too late!

SECURITY TIPS:

- Fit an approved alarm / immobiliser.
- Secure your bike with an approved lock / chain and lock it to an immovable object.
- Use a security marking system.
- During the day, park in a busy, public place.
- At night, park in a well lit area.
- Try to vary the parking place.
- Wherever possible, use custom-built parking places especially ones with fixed stands or security loops.
- Keep a look out for car parks displaying a "Secured Bike Park" sign.
- Cover the machine if possible.
- Always engage the steering lock.
- Get your free copy of the **"Don't give them an easy ride"**, leaflet today!

DON'T GIVE THEM AN EASY RIDE

CRIME
LET'S BRING IT
DOWN

THREE STEPS TO THE FREEDOM OF THE ROAD

STEP 1
Refine your motorcycling skills and pass your test

STEP 2
Select your bike and protective equipment

STEP 3
Check out the best insurance around

- Fantastic Rates
- No forms to fill in
- Immediate Cover
- Instalments
- Breakdown Recovery
- Legal Expenses

MotorCycle Direct M

Call 0870 2410400

Monday to Saturday - 8.30am to 6.00pm

TANGENT
SOUTH WEST
Insurance Services

x1000

30

20

L/100km

MAXIMUM
cover
minimum EFFORT

FREE SECURITY SYSTEM

BREAKDOWN RECOVERY SERVICE

LEGAL COVER

MONTHLY PAYMENT SCHEME

EXPERT ADVICE

FREEPHONE
0800 092 5238/0800 096 1766

UNDERWRITTEN BY A PANEL OF LEADING SPECIALIST INSURANCE COMPANIES AND LLOYDS.
APPOINTED SCHEME MANAGERS FOR *DUCATI* INSURANCE AND
BENELLI INSURANCE

Bikesure
insurance services

low cost
Bike
insurance

08700 771377

open 9.00am to 7.00pm   saturday 9.00am to 4.00pm

This section looks at what to do in the event of an accident.

The questions will ask you about

- **First Aid**

  if you have the knowledge, your fast, effective action might save a life.

- **Warning devices**

  know how to warn other road users of an accident.

- **Reporting procedures**

  know where and when to report an accident.

- **Safety regulations**

  know what to do if a vehicle carrying hazardous loads is involved in an accident.

Question 13.1

Mark one answer

At the scene of an accident you should

- not put yourself at risk
- go to those casualties who are screaming
- pull everybody out of their vehicles
- leave vehicle engines switched on

Answer

not put yourself at risk

It's important that those at the scene of an accident do not create a further risk to themselves or other road users. If the accident has occurred on a motorway, traffic will be approaching at speed. Consider this when trying to help casualties or warn other drivers.

Question 13.2

Mark four answers

You are the first to arrive at the scene of an accident. Which FOUR of these should you do?

- Leave as soon as another motorist arrives
- Switch off the vehicle engine(s)
- Move uninjured people away from the vehicle(s)
- Call the emergency services
- Warn other traffic

Answers

Switch off the vehicle engine(s)

Move uninjured people away from the vehicle(s)

Call the emergency services

Warn other traffic

If you're involved in, or arrive at, the scene of an accident there are certain actions you should take. It's important to know what to do and also what NOT to do. You could save someone's life, or endanger it.

Question 13.3

Mark one answer

An accident has just happened. An injured person is lying in the busy road. What is the FIRST thing you should do to help?

- Treat the person for shock
- Warn other traffic
- Place them in the recovery position
- Make sure the injured person is kept warm

Answer

Warn other traffic

You could do this by

- displaying an advance warning signal, if you have one
- switching on hazard warning lights or other lights
- any other means that does not put you at risk.

Mark three answers

You are the first person to arrive at an accident where people are badly injured. Which THREE should you do?

- Switch on your own hazard warning lights
- Make sure that someone telephones for an ambulance
- Try and get people who are injured to drink something
- Move the people who are injured clear of their vehicles
- Get people who are not injured clear of the scene

Answers

- Switch on your own hazard warning lights
- Make sure that someone telephones for an ambulance
- Get people who are not injured clear of the scene

If you're the first person to arrive at the scene of an accident, further collision and fire are the first concerns. Switching off vehicle engines will reduce the risk of fire. Your hazard warning lights will let approaching traffic know that there's a need for caution.

Don't assume someone else has called the emergency services.

Question 13.5

Mark one answer

You arrive at the scene of a motorcycle accident. The rider is injured. When should the helmet be removed?

- Only when it is essential
- Always straight away
- Only when the motorcyclist asks
- Always, unless they are in shock

Answer

- Only when it is essential

If a motorcyclist has been injured in an accident it's important not to remove their helmet unless it is necessary to keep them alive.

Question 13.6

Mark three answers

You arrive at a serious motorcycle accident. The motorcyclist is unconscious and bleeding. Your main priorities should be to

- try to stop the bleeding
- make a list of witnesses
- check the casualty's breathing
- take the numbers of the vehicles involved
- sweep up any loose debris
- check the casualty's airways

Answers

- try to stop the bleeding
- check the casualty's breathing
- check the casualty's airways

At a road accident the danger of further collisions and fire need to be dealt with first. Injuries should be dealt with in the order

- Airway
- Breathing
- Circulation and bleeding.

Question 13.7

Mark one answer

You arrive at an accident. A motorcyclist is unconscious. Your FIRST priority is the casualty's

■ breathing
■ bleeding
■ broken bones
■ bruising

Answer

■ **breathing**

At the scene of an accident you must first make sure there is no danger from further collisions or fire before dealing with any casualties.

The first priority when dealing with an unconscious person is to make sure they can breathe. This may involve clearing their airway if they're having difficulty or some obstruction is obvious.

Question 13.8

Mark three answers

At an accident a casualty is unconscious. Which THREE of the following should you check urgently?

■ Circulation
■ Airway
■ Shock
■ Breathing
■ Broken bones

Answers

■ **Circulation**
■ **Airway**
■ **Breathing**

An unconscious casualty may have difficulty breathing. Check that their tongue has not fallen back, blocking their airway. Do this by tilting the head back slightly.

Question 13.9

Mark three answers

You arrive at the scene of an accident. It has just happened and someone is unconscious. Which of the following should be given urgent priority to help them?

■ Clear the airway and keep it open
■ Try to get them to drink water
■ Check that they are breathing
■ Look for any witnesses
■ Stop any heavy bleeding
■ Take the numbers of vehicles involved

Answers

■ **Clear the airway and keep it open**
■ **Check that they are breathing**
■ **Stop any heavy bleeding**

Stay with the casualty and send someone to ring for an ambulance.

Mark three answers

At an accident someone is unconscious. Your main priorities should be to

▓ sweep up the broken glass

▓ take the names of witnesses

▓ count the number of vehicles involved

▓ check the airway is clear

▓ make sure they are breathing

▓ stop any heavy bleeding

Answers

▓ **check the airway is clear**

▓ **make sure they are breathing**

▓ **stop any heavy bleeding**

Remember this procedure by saying ABC. Airway – Breathing – Circulation

Mark three answers

You have stopped at the scene of an accident to give help. Which THREE things should you do?

▓ Keep injured people warm and comfortable

▓ Keep injured people calm by talking to them reassuringly

▓ Keep injured people on the move by walking them around

▓ Give injured people a warm drink

▓ Make sure that injured people are not left alone

Answers

▓ **Keep injured people warm and comfortable**

▓ **Keep injured people calm by talking to them reassuringly**

▓ **Make sure that injured people are no left alone**

If you stop at the scene of an accident to give help and there are casualties don't

• move injured people, unless further danger is threatened

• give the injured anything to drink.

Mark three answers

You arrive at the scene of an accident. It has just happened and someone is injured. Which THREE of the following should be given urgent priority?

▓ Stop any severe bleeding

▓ Get them a warm drink

▓ Check that their breathing is OK

▓ Take numbers of vehicles involved

▓ Look for witnesses

▓ Clear their airway and keep it open

Answers

▓ **Stop any severe bleeding**

▓ **Check that their breathing is OK**

▓ **Clear their airway and keep it open**

When you have done this, call the emergenc services; they are the experts.

If you feel you are not capable of carrying ou first aid, then consider doing some training. It could save a life.

DSA **THEORY TEST** for motorcyclist

Question 13.13

Mark two answers

At an accident a casualty has stopped breathing. You should

▪ remove anything that is blocking the mouth

▪ keep the head tilted forwards as far as possible

▪ raise the legs to help with circulation

▪ try to give the casualty something to drink

▪ keep the head tilted back as far as possible

Answers

▪ **remove anything that is blocking the mouth**

▪ **keep the head tilted back as far as possible**

These actions will ensure that the casualty has clear airways and is in the correct position if mouth to mouth ventilation is required.

Question 13.14

Mark four answers

You are at the scene of an accident. Someone is suffering from shock. You should

▪ reassure them constantly

▪ offer them a cigarette

▪ keep them warm

▪ avoid moving them if possible

▪ loosen any tight clothing

▪ give them a warm drink

Answers

▪ **reassure them constantly**

▪ **keep them warm**

▪ **avoid moving them if possible**

▪ **loosen any tight clothing**

The effects of trauma may not be immediately obvious. Prompt treatment can help to minimise the effects of shock.

• lay the casualty down

• loosen tight clothing

• call an ambulance

• check their breathing and pulse.

Mark one answer

Which of the following should you NOT do at the scene of an accident?

- Warn other traffic by switching on your hazard warning lights
- Call the emergency services immediately
- Offer someone a cigarette to calm them down
- Ask drivers to switch off their engines

Answer

- **Offer someone a cigarette to calm them down**

Keeping casualties or witnesses calm is important, but never offer a cigarette becau of the risk of fire. Check for any signs of shock, such as,

- sweating
- clammy skin
- giddiness
- rapid or shallow breathing
- a weak pulse.

Mark two answers

There has been an accident. The driver is suffering from shock. You should

- give them a drink
- reassure them
- not leave them alone
- offer them a cigarette
- ask who caused the accident

Answers

- **reassure them**
- **not leave them alone**

They could have an injury that is not immediately obvious. Loosen any tight clothing and check that their breathing is nc rapid or slow.

Mark three answers

You are at the scene of an accident. Someone is suffering from shock. You should

- offer them a cigarette
- offer them a warm drink
- keep them warm
- loosen any tight clothing
- reassure them constantly

Answers

- **keep them warm**
- **loosen any tight clothing**
- **reassure them constantly**

People who seem to be unhurt may be suffering from shock. Try to reassure everyone involved at the scene and keep everybody calm.

Question 13.18

Mark one answer

You have to treat someone for shock at the scene of an accident. You should

- reassure them constantly
- walk them around to calm them down
- give them something cold to drink
- cool them down as soon as possible

Answer

reassure them constantly

You should lay the casualty down and loosen any tight clothing, whilst reassuring them. If possible, get someone else to call an ambulance to avoid leaving the casualty alone.

Question 13.19

Mark one answer

You arrive at the scene of a motorcycle accident. No other vehicle is involved. The rider is unconscious, lying in the middle of the road. The first thing you should do is

- move the rider out of the road
- warn other traffic
- clear the road of debris
- give the rider reassurance

Answer

warn other traffic

The motorcyclist is in an extremely vulnerable position, exposed to further danger from traffic. The traffic needs to slow right down and be aware of the hazard in good time.

Question 13.20

Mark one answer

At an accident a small child is not breathing. When giving mouth to mouth you should breathe

- sharply
- gently
- heavily
- rapidly

Answer

gently

With a small child breathe gently into the nose and mouth until you see the chest rise.

Mark three answers

To start mouth to mouth on a casualty you should

- tilt their head forward
- clear the airway
- turn them on their side
- tilt their head back
- pinch the nostrils together
- put their arms across their chest

Answer

- clear the airway
- tilt their head back
- pinch the nostrils together

Use your finger to check for and move any obvious obstruction in the mouth. It's important to ensure that the airways are clear

---

Question 13.22

Mark one answer

When you are giving mouth to mouth you should only stop when

- you think the casualty is dead
- the casualty can breathe without help
- the casualty has turned blue
- you think the ambulance is coming

Answer

- the casualty can breathe without help

Don't give up. Look for signs of recovery and check the casualty's pulse. When the casualty starts to breathe, place them in the recovery position.

Question 13.23

Mark one answer

You arrive at the scene of an accident. There has been an engine fire and someone's hands and arms have been burnt. You should NOT

- douse the burn thoroughly with cool liquid
- lay the casualty down
- remove anything sticking to the burn
- reassure them constantly

Answer

- remove anything sticking to the burn

This could cause further damage and infection to the wound. Your first priorities are to cool the burn and check the patient for shock.

Question 13.24

Mark one answer

You arrive at an accident where someone is suffering from severe burns. You should

- apply lotions to the injury
- burst any blisters
- remove anything stuck to the burns
- douse the burns with cool liquid

Answer

■ **douse the burns with cool liquid**

Try to find fluid that is clean, cold and non-toxic. Its coolness will stop the burn and relieve the pain. Keep the wound doused for at least ten minutes. If blisters appear don't attempt to burst them as this could lead to infection.

Question 13.25

Mark one answer

You arrive at an accident where someone is suffering from severe burns. You should

- burst any blisters
- douse the burns thoroughly with cool liquid
- apply lotions to the injury
- remove anything sticking to the burns

Answer

■ **douse the burns thoroughly with cool liquid**

Do this for about ten minutes, making sure that the casualty is comfortable. If any clothing is stuck to the wound, don't try to remove it.

Question 13.26

Mark two answers

You arrive at the scene of an accident. A pedestrian has a severe bleeding wound on their leg, although it is not broken. What should you do?

- Dab the wound to stop bleeding
- Keep both legs flat on the ground
- Apply firm pressure to the wound
- Raise the leg to lessen bleeding
- Fetch them a warm drink

Answer

■ **Apply firm pressure to the wound**

■ **Raise the leg to lessen bleeding**

As soon as you can, apply a pad to the wound with a bandage or a clean length of cloth. Raising the leg will lessen the flow of blood. Be aware that any restriction of blood circulation for more than a short period of time may result in long-term injury.

Mark one answer

You arrive at the scene of an accident. A passenger is bleeding badly from an arm wound. What should you do?

- ▓ Apply pressure over the wound and keep the arm down
- ▓ Dab the wound
- ▓ Get them a drink
- ▓ Apply pressure over the wound and raise the arm

Answer

▓ **Apply pressure over the wound and raise the arm**

If possible, lay the casualty down. Raising t[ ]arm above the level of the heart will stem t[ ]flow of blood.

Mark one answer

You arrive at the scene of an accident. A pedestrian is bleeding heavily from a leg wound, but the leg is not broken. What should you do?

- ▓ Dab the wound to stop the bleeding
- ▓ Keep both legs flat on the ground
- ▓ Apply firm pressure to the wound
- ▓ Fetch them a warm drink

Answer

▓ **Apply firm pressure to the wound**

Lift the casualty's leg so that the wound is higher than their heart. This should reduce the flow of blood.

Mark one answer

At an accident a casualty is unconscious but still breathing. You should only move them if

- ▓ an ambulance is on its way
- ▓ bystanders advise you to
- ▓ there is further danger
- ▓ bystanders will help you to

Answer

▓ **there is further danger**

Moving them could cause further injury, so it's important that this is only done if there is obvious danger to the casualty.

Question 13.30

Mark one answer

At an accident you suspect a casualty has back injuries. The area is safe. You should

- offer them a drink
- not move them
- raise their legs
- offer them a cigarette

Answer

 not move them

Talk to the casualty and keep them calm. If you attempt to move them it could cause further injury. Call an ambulance at the first opportunity.

Question 13.31

Mark one answer

At an accident it is important to look after the casualty. When the area is safe, you should

- get them out of the vehicle
- give them a drink
- give them something to eat
- keep them in the vehicle

Answer

keep them in the vehicle

Don't move casualties who are trapped in vehicles unless they are in danger.

Question 13.32

Mark one answer

A tanker is involved in an accident. Which sign would show that the tanker is carrying dangerous goods?

Answer

2YE 1089 Newtown-on-Moors 0181 645 2830

There will be an orange label on the side and rear of the lorry. Look at this carefully and report what it says when you phone the emergency services.

Mark two answers

For which TWO should you use hazard warning lights?

▆ When you slow down quickly on a motorway because of a hazard ahead

▆ When you have broken down

▆ When you wish to stop on double yellow lines

▆ When you need to park on the pavement

Answers

▆ **When you slow down quickly on a motorway because of a hazard ahead**

▆ **When you have broken down**

Hazard warning lights are fitted to all modern cars and some motorcycles. They should be used to warn other road users of a hazard ahead.

Mark three answers

For which THREE should you use your hazard warning lights?

▆ When you are parking in a restricted area

▆ When you are temporarily obstructing traffic

▆ To warn following traffic of a hazard ahead

▆ When you have broken down

▆ When only stopping for a short time

Answers

▆ **When you are temporarily obstructing traffic**

▆ **To warn following traffic of a hazard ahead**

▆ **When you have broken down**

Use them on the motorway when you have to slow down suddenly because of a queue of traffic ahead. This is to warn following traffic that you're slowing suddenly and rapidly.

Mark one answer

When are you allowed to use hazard warning lights?

▆ When stopped and temporarily obstructing traffic

▆ When travelling during darkness without headlights

▆ When parked for shopping on double yellow lines

▆ When travelling slowly because you are lost

Answer

▆ **When stopped and temporarily obstructing traffic**

Don't use hazard lights

• to excuse yourself for illegal, dangerous or inconsiderate parking

• when you're moving slowly because you're lost

• when you're moving slowly due to bad weather.

Question 13.36

Mark one answer

Your motorcycle has broken down on a motorway. How will you know the direction of the nearest emergency telephone?

- By walking with the flow of traffic
- By following an arrow on a marker post
- By walking against the flow of traffic
- By remembering where the last phone was

Answer

By following an arrow on a marker post

If you break down on a motorway you should

- pull onto the hard shoulder and stop as far over to the left as you can
- switch on hazard lights (if they are fitted)
- make your way to the nearest emergency telephone.

Marker posts spaced every 100 metres will direct you to the nearest telephone.

Question 13.37

Mark three answers

The police may ask you to produce which three of these documents following an accident?

- Vehicle registration document
- Driving licence
- Theory test certificate
- Insurance certificate
- MOT test certificate
- Road tax disc

Answers

Driving licence

Insurance certificate

MOT test certificate

The first thing you must do is stop. It is an offence not to do so.

Mark four answers

You are involved in an accident with a driver. Someone is injured. Your motorcycle is damaged. Which FOUR of the following should you find out?

- ▪ Whether the driver owns the other vehicle involved
- ▪ The other driver's name, address and telephone number
- ▪ The car make and registration number of the other vehicle
- ▪ The occupation of the other driver
- ▪ The details of the other driver's vehicle insurance
- ▪ Whether the other driver is licensed to drive

Answer

- ▪ Whether the driver owns the other vehicle involved
- ▪ The other driver's name, address and telephone number
- ▪ The car make and registration numbe of the other vehicle
- ▪ The details of the other driver's vehicle insurance

Try to keep calm and don't rush the proceedings. Take your time. You might be a little shaken by the incident, but try to ensure that you have all the details before you leave the scene.

Question 13.39

Mark one answer

At a railway level crossing the red light signal continues to flash after a train has gone by. What should you do?

- ▪ Phone the signal operator
- ▪ Alert drivers behind you
- ▪ Wait
- ▪ Proceed with caution

Answer

- ▪ Wait

Don't

- proceed
- phone the signal operator immediately
- zigzag between the gates.

There may be another train coming.

Question 13.40

Mark one answer

You should use the engine cut-out switch to

- ▪ stop the engine in an emergency
- ▪ stop the engine on short journeys
- ▪ save wear on the ignition switch
- ▪ start the engine if you lose the key

Answer

- ▪ stop the engine in an emergency

Most motorcycles are fitted with an engine cut-out switch. This is designed to stop the engine in an emergency and so reduce the risk of fire.

DSA THEORY TEST for motorcyclist

Question 13.41

Mark one answer

You see a car on the hard shoulder of a motorway with a HELP pennant displayed. This means the driver is most likely to be

- a disabled person
- first aid trained
- a foreign visitor
- a rescue patrol person

Answer

- **a disabled person**

The driver might not be able to walk the distance to the emergency telephone. Disabled persons can show this sign to alert police controls.

Question 13.42

Mark one answer

On the motorway the hard shoulder should be used

- to answer a mobile phone
- when an emergency arises
- for a short rest when tired
- to check a road atlas

Answer

- **when an emergency arises**

Pull onto the hard shoulder and use the emergency telephone to report your problem. The telephone connects you to police control, who will put you through to an emergency breakdown service. Never cross the carriageway to use a telephone on the other side.

Question 13.43

Mark three answers

You have broken down on a motorway. When you use the emergency telephone you will be asked

- for the number on the telephone that you are using
- for your driving licence details
- for the name of your vehicle insurance company
- for details of yourself and your vehicle
- whether you belong to a motoring organisation

Answers

- **for the number on the telephone that you are using**
- **for details of yourself and your vehicle**
- **whether you belong to a motoring organisation**

Have these details ready before you phone to save time. Be sure to give the correct information. It is safer to always face the traffic when you speak on the telephone.

Question 13.44

Mark one answer

You are on the motorway. Luggage falls from your motorcycle. What should you do?

- Stop at the next emergency telephone and contact the police

- Stop on the motorway and put on hazard lights whilst you pick it up

- Walk back up the motorway to pick it up

- Pull up on the hard shoulder and wave traffic down

Answer

■ **Stop at the next emergency telephone and contact the police**

Pull over onto the hard shoulder near an emergency telephone and phone for assistance. Don't

- stop on the carriageway
- attempt to retrieve anything.

Question 13.45

Mark one answer

You are travelling on a motorway. A bag falls from your motorcycle. There are valuables in the bag. What should you do?

- Go back carefully and collect the bag as quickly as possible

- Stop wherever you are and pick up the bag, but only when there is a safe gap

- Stop on the hard shoulder and use the emergency telephone to inform the police

- Stop on the hard shoulder and then retrieve the bag yourself

Answer

■ **Stop on the hard shoulder and use the emergency telephone to inform the police**

However important you think retrieving your property may be, DON'T walk onto the motorway. Your bag might be creating a hazard, but not as great a hazard as you would be.

Question 13.46

Mark one answer

You are on a motorway. A large box falls onto the road from a lorry. The lorry does not stop. You should

- go to the next emergency telephone and inform the police

- catch up with the lorry and try to get the driver's attention

- stop close to the box until the police arrive

- pull over to the hard shoulder, then remove the box

Answer

■ **go to the next emergency telephone and inform the police**

Lorry drivers are sometimes unaware of objects falling from their vehicles. If you see something fall off a lorry onto the motorway watch to see if the driver pulls over. If the lorry doesn't stop, you should

- pull over onto the hard shoulder near an emergency telephone
- report the hazard to the police.

Question 13.47

Mark two answers

You are on a motorway. When can you use hazard warning lights?

- [ ] When a vehicle is following too closely
- [ ] When you slow down quickly because of danger ahead
- [ ] When you are being towed by another vehicle
- [ ] When riding on the hard shoulder
- [ ] When you have broken down on the hard shoulder

Question 13.48

Mark one answer

You are on a motorway. The car in front switches on its hazard warning lights whilst moving. This means

- [ ] they are going to take the next exit
- [ ] there is a danger ahead
- [ ] there is a police car in the left lane
- [ ] they are trying to change lanes

Answers

- [x] **When you slow down quickly because of danger ahead**
- [x] **When you have broken down on the hard shoulder**

Hazard lights will warn the traffic travelling behind you that your motorcycle is a potential hazard. Don't forget to turn them off again when you return to the carriageway or normal speed.

Answer

- [x] **there is a danger ahead**

Hazard lights should only be used when riding if you're on a

- motorway
- dual carriageway subject to the national speed limit

and you need to warn following traffic of a danger ahead.

This section looks at the safety of loads.

The questions will ask you about

- **Stability**

  make sure that you carry pillion passengers and luggage safely.

- **Towing regulations**

  be aware of the effects of towing a trailer and the rules that apply.

Question 14.1

Mark two answers

Overloading your motorcycle can seriously affect the

- gearbox
- steering
- handling
- battery life
- journey time

Answers

- steering
- handling

Any load will have an affect on the handling of your motorcycle, this becomes worse if you overload it. Any change in the centre of gravity or weight the motorcycle is carrying will affect it's handling on bends.

Question 14.2

Mark one answer

Who is responsible for making sure that a motorcycle is not overloaded?

- The rider of the motorcycle
- The owner of the items being carried
- The person who loaded the motorcycle
- The owner of the motorcycle

Answer

- The rider of the motorcycle

Your motorcycle must not be overloaded. This will affect control and handling characteristics. If your motorcycle is overloaded and it causes an accident, you'll be responsible.

Question 14.3

Mark one answer

Any load that is carried on a luggage rack MUST be

- securely fastened when riding
- carried only when strictly necessary
- visible when you are riding
- covered with plastic sheeting

Answer

- securely fastened when riding

Don't risk losing any luggage off your motorcycle. It could fall into the path of following vehicles and cause danger. It's an offence to travel with an insecure load.

Mark one answer

You want to tow a trailer with your motorcycle. Which one applies?

- The motorcycle should be attached to a sidecar
- The trailer should weigh more than the motorcycle
- The trailer should be fitted with brakes
- The trailer should not be more than 1 metre (3 feet 3 inches) wide

Answer

- **The trailer should not be more than 1 metre (3 feet 3 inches) wide**

To tow a trailer behind a motorcycle you must

- have a full motorcycle licence
- have a motorcycle with an engine larger than 125 cc.

Motorcycle trailers must not exceed 1 metre (3 feet 3 inches) in width.

Mark one answer

If a trailer swerves or snakes when you are towing it you should

- ease off the throttle and reduce your speed
- let go of the handlebars and let it correct itself
- brake hard and hold the brake on
- increase your speed as quickly as possible

Answer

- **ease off the throttle and reduce your speed**

Don't be tempted to use the steering to stop swerving or snaking. This won't help the situation. Ease off the throttle and reduce your speed.

Mark two answers

You are towing a small trailer on a busy three-lane motorway. All the lanes are open. You must

- not exceed 60 mph
- not overtake
- have a stabiliser fitted
- use only the left and centre lanes

Answers

- **not exceed 60 mph**
- **use only the left and centre lanes**

You should be aware of the speed limit for the motorcycle that you're riding. Allow the faster-moving traffic to flow. Don't use the right-hand lane.

Question 14.7

Mark one answer

You have a side-car fitted to your motorcycle. What effect will it have?

- Reduce stability
- Make steering lighter
- Increase stopping distance
- Increase fuel economy

Answer

Increase stopping distance

If you want to fit a sidecar to your motorcycle

- make sure that your motorcycle is suitable to cope with the extra load
- make sure that the sidecar is fixed correctly and properly aligned.

A sidecar will affect the handling of your motorcycle. Give yourself time to adjust to the different characteristics.

Question 14.8

Mark two answers

When riding with a sidecar attached for the first time you should

- keep your speed down
- be able to stop more quickly
- accelerate quickly round bends
- approach corners more carefully

Answers

keep your speed down

approach corners more carefully

A motorcycle with a sidecar will feel very different to ride than a solo motorcycle. Until you get used to the outfit keep your speed down especially when negotiating corners and bends.

Question 14.9

Mark one answer

A trailer on a motorcycle must be no wider than

- 1 metre (3 feet 3 inches)
- 1/2 metre (1 foot 8 inches)
- 1 1/2 metres (4 feet 11inches)
- 2 metres (6 feet 6 inches)

Answer

1 metre (3 feet 3 inches)

When you're towing a trailer you must remember that you may not be able to filter through traffic. Don't 'forget' that the trailer is there.

Question 14.10

Mark one answer

Before fitting a side-car riders should

- have the wheels of their motorcycle balanced
- have their motorcycle's engine tuned
- pass the extended motorcycle test
- check that their motorcycle is suitable

Answer

check that their motorcycle is suitable

Make sure that the sidecar is fixed and is properly aligned. If your motorcycle is registered on or after 1 August 1981 the sidecar must be fitted on the left side of the motorcycle.

Question 14.11

Mark two answers

You want to tow a trailer behind your motorcycle. You should

- display a 'long vehicle' sign
- fit a larger battery
- have a full motorcycle licence
- ensure that your engine is more than 125 cc
- ensure that your motorcycle has shaft drive

Answer

have a full motorcycle licence

ensure that your engine is more than 125 cc

When you tow a trailer

- your stopping distance may be increased
- any load on the trailer must be secure
- the trailer must be fitted to the motorcycle correctly
- you must obey the speed limit restrictions that apply to all vehicles with trailers.

Question 14.12

Mark one answer

When may a learner motorcyclist carry a pillion passenger?

- If the passenger holds a full licence
- Not at any time
- If the rider is undergoing training
- If the passenger is over 21

Answer

Not at any time

You are not allowed to carry a pillion passenger until you hold a full motorcycle licence.

This allows you to gain experience riding solo before carrying a passenger.

DSA THEORY TEST for motorcyclists

Question 14.13

Mark three answers

Which THREE must a learner motorcyclist under 21 NOT do?

- Ride a motorcycle with an engine capacity greater than 125 cc
- Pull a trailer
- Carry a pillion passenger
- Ride faster than 30 mph
- Use the right-hand lane on dual carriageways

Answer

- **Ride a motorcycle with an engine capacity greater than 125 cc**
- **Pull a trailer**
- **Carry a pillion passenger**

If you're a learner motorcyclist under 21 you must not ride a motorcycle on the road with an engine capacity over 125 cc.

Question 14.14

Mark one answer

Pillion passengers should

- have a provisional motorcycle licence
- be lighter than the rider
- always wear a helmet
- signal for the rider

Answer

- **always wear a helmet**

Pillion passengers must

- sit astride the machine facing forward on a proper passenger seat
- wear a safety helmet, which is correctly fastened.

Question 14.15

Mark one answer

Pillion passengers should

- give the rider directions
- lean with the rider when going round bends
- check the road behind for the rider
- give arm signals for the rider

Answer

- **lean with the rider when going round bends**

Pillion passengers should also keep both feet on the pillion footrests provided.

Mark three answers

When carrying extra weight on a motorcycle, you may need to make adjustments to the

- headlight
- gears
- suspension
- tyres
- footrests

Answers

- headlight
- suspension
- tyres

Extra weight can affect a motorcycles feel and balance. To help, you can adjust the

- suspension
- tyre pressures.

You may find extra weight on the back affects the headlamp aim, and this can be adjusted to compensate.

Mark two answers

To carry a pillion passenger your motorcycle should be fitted with

- rear footrests
- an engine of 250cc or over
- a top box
- a grab handle
- a proper passenger seat

Answer

- rear footrests
- a proper passenger seat

Pillion passengers should be instructed not to

- give hand signals
- lean away from the rider when cornering
- fidget or move around
- put their feet down to try and support the machine as you stop
- wear long, loose items that might get caught in the rear wheel or drive chain.

Question 14.18

Mark one answer

To obtain the full category 'A' licence through the accelerated or direct access scheme, your motorcycle must be

- solo with maximum power 25 kw (33 bhp)
- solo with maximum power of 11 kw (14.6 bhp)
- fitted with a sidecar and have minimum power of 35 kw (46.6 bhp)
- solo with minimum power of 35 kw (46.6 bhp)

Answer

- **solo with minimum power of 35 kw (46.6 bhp)**

If you want to ride in countries who are members of the European Community you must have a valid driving licence. You will also want to find out what specific rules apply to any country you may be visiting concerning insurance, visas and other motoring regulations.

Question 14.19

Mark one answer

When you are going around a corner your pillion passenger should

- give arm signals for you
- check behind for other vehicles
- lean with you on bends
- lean to one side to see ahead

Answer

- **lean with you on bends**

A pillion passenger should not give signals or look round for you. They should lean with you when going around bends and corners so that you can maintain balance and stability.

Question 14.20

Mark one answer

Which of these may need to be adjusted when carrying a pillion passenger?

- Indicators
- Exhaust
- Fairing
- Headlight

Answer

- **Headlight**

Lights must be properly adjusted to prevent dazzling other road users. Extra attention needs to be paid to this if the motorcycle is heavily loaded. This is important when carrying the extra weight of a pillion passenger which will mean that the motorcycle will become lower at the back and cause the headlight to shine higher.

Mark three answers

Your motorcycle is fitted with a top box. It is unwise to carry a heavy load in the top box because it may

- reduce stability
- improve stability
- make turning easier
- cause high-speed weave
- cause low-speed wobble
- increase fuel economy

Answers

- **reduce stability**
- **cause high-speed weave**
- **cause low-speed wobble**

Because the weight is high up and over the rear wheel it can cause problems in maintaining control of the motorcycle.

Mark one answer

You are towing a trailer with your motorcycle. You should remember that your

- stopping distance may increase
- fuel consumption will improve
- tyre grip will increase
- stability will improve

Answer

- **stopping distance may increase**

When you tow a trailer remember that

- you must obey the speed limits
- your stopping distance will increase
- the trailer must be hitched correctly.

Above all, **don't forget it's there**.

Service standards for theory test candidates

DSA and DVTA are committed to providing the following standards of service for test candidates.

1   Following routing by our call handling systems, ninety percent of telephone calls will be answered within twenty seconds.

2   Theory tests will be available during weekdays, evenings and on Saturdays. A test appointment should be available for 95% of test candidates within two weeks.

3   99% of test notifications will be issued within five working days of receipt of a correctly completed application form and appropriate fee.

4   More time may be needed to make arrangements for candidates with special needs, but a test should be available for 95% of such candidates within four weeks.

5   99.8% of all candidates should be able to obtain a test booking within two months of their preferred date at the centre of their choice.

6   A refund of test fees will be issued within three weeks of a valid claim with the supporting information.

7   No more than 0.5% of tests will be cancelled by contractors (acting on behalf of DSA and DVTA).

8   All letters, including complaints, will be answered within 15 working days.

9   98% of all candidates should receive their test result within 30 minutes of completing their test.

Complaints guide for theory test candidates

DSA and DVTA aim to give their customers the best possible service. Please tell us

* when we've done well
* when you aren't satisfied.

Your comments can help us to improve the service we offer. If you have any questions about your theory test please contact DSA.

Tel: 0870 01 01 372

Fax: 0870 01 04 372.

Candidates with comments or queries about tests in Northern Ireland please contact DVTA.

Tel: 0845 6006700

Fax: 0870 01 04 372.

If you have any complaints about how your theory test was carried out, or any part of our customer service, please take up the matter with a member of staff if the circumstances allow. Alternatively you can write to the Customer Services Manager at the following address

Customer Services
Driving Theory Test
PO Box 148
Salford
M5 3SY

If you're dissatisfied with the reply you can write to the Managing Director at the same address.

If you're still not satisfied, you can take up your complaint with

The Chief Executive
Driving Standards Agency
56 Stanley House
Talbot Street
Nottingham NG1 5GU.

In Northern Ireland

The Chief Executive
Driver & Vehicle Testing Agency
Balmoral Road
Belfast BT12 6QL.

None of this removes your right to take your complaint to your Member of Parliament, who may decide to raise your case personally with the DSA or DVTA Chief Executive, the Minister or the Parliamentary Commissioner for Administration (the Ombudsman). Please refer to our leaflet 'If things go wrong.'

FURTHER INFORMATION

Compensation code for theory test candidates

DSA will normally refund the test fee, or give a free re-booking, in the following cases

- if we cancel your test
- if you cancel and give us at least three clear working days notice
- if you keep the test appointment but the test doesn't take place, or isn't finished, for a reason that isn't your fault.

We'll also repay you the expenses that you incurred on the day of the test because we cancelled your test at short notice. We'll consider reasonable claims for

- travelling to and from the test centre
- any pay or earnings you lost after tax (usually for half a day).

Please write to the address below and send a receipt showing travel costs and/or an employer's letter, which shows what earnings you lost.

DVTA has a different compensation code. If you think you're entitled to compensation write to

Customer Services
Driving Theory Test
PO Box 148
Salford
M5 3SY

This compensation code doesn't affect your existing legal rights.

DSA THEORY TEST for car drivers and motorcyclists

Theory Test Centres in Great Britain and Northern Ireland

Scotland

Aberdeen
Ayr
Berwick-Upon-Tweed
Dumfries
Dundee
Dunfermline
Edinburgh
Elgin
Fort William
Gairloch
Galashiels
Glasgow NW
Glasgow Central
Greenock
Helmsdale
Huntly
Inverness
Isle of Arran
Isle of Barra
Isle of Benbecula
Isle of Islay, Bowmore
Isle of Mull, Salen
Isle of Tiree
Kirkwall
Kyle of Lochalsh
Lerwick
Motherwell
Oban
Pitlochry
Portree
Stirling
Stornoway
Stranraer
Tarbert, Argyllshire
Tongue
Ullapool
Wick

Northern

Barrow
Birkenhead
Blackpool
Bolton
Bradford
Carlisle
Chester
Doncaster
Durham
Grimsby
Harrogate
Huddersfield
Hull
Leeds
Liverpool
Manchester
Middlesbrough
Morpeth
Newcastle
Oldham
Preston
Runcorn
Salford
Scarborough
Scunthorpe
Sheffield
Southport
St Helens
Stockport
Sunderland
Wigan
Workington
York

Midlands & Eastern

Birmingham
Boston
Bury St Edmunds
Cambridge
Chesterfield
Coventry
Derby
Dudley
Grantham
Ipswich
Kings Lynn
Leicester
Lincoln
Lowestoft
Luton
Mansfield
Milton Keynes
Northampton
Norwich
Nottingham
Oxford
Peterborough
Reading
Redditch
Shrewsbury
Solihull
Stoke-on-Trent
Stratford Upon Avon
Sutton Coldfield
Wolverhampton
Worcester

FURTHER INFORMATION

Wales & Western

Aberystwyth
Bangor
Barnstaple
Basingstoke
Bath
Bournemouth
Bristol
Builth Wells
Cardiff
Cheltenham
Exeter
Fareham
Gloucester
Haverfordwest
Hereford
Isles of Scilly
Isle of Wight
Merthyr Tydfil
Newport
Penzance
Plymouth
Portsmouth
Rhyl
Swansea
Salisbury
Southampton
Swindon
Taunton
Torquay
Truro
Weymouth
Yeovil

London & South East

Aldershot
Basildon
Brighton
Canterbury
Chelmsford
Colchester
Crawley
Croydon
Eastbourne
Gillingham
Guildford
Harlow
Hastings
Ilford
Kingston
Palmers Green
Sidcup
Slough
Southend
Southwark
Staines
Stevenage
Uxbridge
Watford
Worthing

Northern Ireland

Ballymena
Belfast
Londonderry
Newry
Omagh
Portadown

DSA THEORY TEST for car drivers and motorcyclists

A & S Motorcycle Centre

We are a small and friendly motorcycle business who can offer you everything you need for your motorcycle.

- Full service and repair facilities
- MoT Testing Centre
- Spares and accessories shop
- Clothes, leathers, helmets, boots, etc
- New and second hand motorcycles for sale
- Mail order service – usually next day delivery
- Major credit cards accepted
- Finance can be arranged (subject to status)

16c Cowleigh Road, Malvern, Worcestershire. WR14 1QD

Telephone
01684 565630 or **0403 857170**

Fax
01684 565630

Email: sally@asmotorcyclecentre.fsnet.co.uk
www.asmotorcyclecentre.fsnet.co.uk

 Enjoy you motorcycling – with A & S Motorcycle Centre

CHECK
03457 58 53 50
FIRST!

Motorcycle
Rider Training
Association

Motorcycle
Retailers
Association

By dealing with a member of the Motorcycle Retailers Association (MRA) or the Motorcycle Rider Training Association (MRTA) you have the right to complain to us if things go wrong.

Whether it is to do with buying a new or used motorcycle, or undertaking rider training, membership is all about maintaining high standards.

Our members must comply with a strict Motorcycle Code of Practice and co-operate with our National Conciliation Service when faced with a customer complaint.
It's a condition of membership.

Please contact our Motorline on
03457 58 53 50

(local rates), to find our names of members in your area.

Remember, we cannot help you unless it was a member you dealt with!

ROTALOK®SECURITY

THE BEST QUALITY SECURITY PRODUCTS AVAILABLE – GUARANTEED

UNIQUE LIFETIME GUARANTEE

TESTED AND APPROVED BY:
● *MOD* ● *HSE EXPLOSIVES* ● *LOS PREVENTION COUNCIL* ● *SOLD SECURE*
TO ORDER TEL 01928 566664 OR FAX 01928 563051
CATCH US ON THE INTERNET @ http://www.rotalok.com
EMAIL US @ sales@rotalok.com

ALSO AVAILABLE
A new concept in security, ***total surprise***, sending a *silent*
warning message to you, without alerting the thief.

SILENT WARNING is a totally independent paging system,
integrated with its own movement sensors for detection. When an
attempt is made to steal the bike the transmitter will activate and
send a silent signal to the mini receiver you are carrying in your
pocket, alerting you, but leaving the intruder unaware.

11 ACRE PRIVATE ROAD

TRAINING CENTRE

NON CAR PARK ENVIRONMENT	BUILD YOUR CONFIDENCE	UNDERAGE RIDERS ENVIRONMENT

BEGINNERS:- 2 DAYS ON 125CC + 3 DAYS ON 500CC ON 5 DAY DIRECT ACCESS COURSES

- CBT EVERYDAY INC. SUNDAY •
- DIRECT ACCESS COURSES •
- LATEST BIKES, SCOOTERS & MOPEDS •
- 11 ACRES OF PRIVATE ROADS •
- UNBEATABLE FACILITIES •

OPEN 7 DAYS A WEEK

01621 851679

THE CARDROME, UPPER RAINHAM RD, HORNCHURCH, ESSEX

ALSO AT: THE ROAD SAFETY CENTRE,
EDINBURGH WAY, HARLOW, ESSEX
ALSO AT 306 STAFFORD ROAD
CROYDON
(0208 688 5200)

Matchless Rider Training

DSA THEORY TEST for motorcyclists

DSA THEORY TEST for motorcyclists

DSA THEORY TEST **for motorcyclists**

Essential Reading

The Highway Code

The latest Highway Code has been completely revised to include new legislation, with greater emphasis on safe driving and special sections on vulnerable road users such as horse riders, cyclists and the elderly. Plus advice to reflect the changes in lifestyle and technology, with rules dealing with driver fatigue and recommendations about the use of mobile phones.

ISBN 0 11 551977 7   £1.49

Know Your Traffic Signs

This useful publication illustrates and explains the vast majority of traffic signals, signs and road markings which any road user is likely to encounter. It is the most comprehensive explanation of the signing system available, and is exceptional value for money.

ISBN 0 11 551612 3   £2.50

The Official Driving Test

Written by the people who set and conduct the practical test – DSA – this book will give you essential guidance on how to prepare for the test and what to do and not to do during the test.

ISBN 0 11 552190 9   £6.99

The Official Driving Manual

Also written by DSA, this book give you excellent all-round advice on practical driving skills, basic maintenance, first aid, driving abroad and emergencies. Almost everything you need to be prepared for your test and beyond.

ISBN 0 11 552191 7   £12.99

The Official Motorcycling Manual

he authoritative guide to motorcycling,
ontaining new graphics and photographs
nd updated to include the very latest
nformation and advice. An essential
eference book for motorcyclists who
re keen to improve their machine
andling and safety skills, including
xpert guidance on riding in traffic,
efensive driving, in bad weather
nd at night.

11 552193 3   £9.99

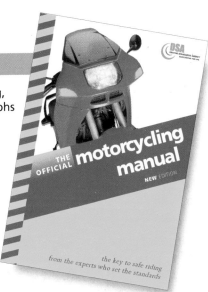

The Official Compulsory Basic Training for Motorcyclists

pdated to include all the information
or the first step for motorcycle learners.
BT is the course that you must complete
efore riding a moped or motorcycle.
his title, written and compiled by the
SA explains each of the various
lements of the training, with helpful
nformation for pre and post course
ssistance.

11 552192 5   £9.99

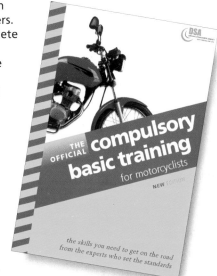

Order Form

TSO publications are available from:

- **Mail Order:**
  The Stationery Office, PO Box 29, Norwich NR3 1GN
- **Tel:** 0870 600 5522 *quoting ref ASX*
  Fax: 0870 600 5533
  Online: www.**clicktso**.com
- **The Stationery Office Bookshops**
  (See inside back cover for details)
- **Accredited Agents and all good booksellers**

Please send me the following publications:

Title	ISBN	Price	Quantity
The Highway Code	0 11 551977 7	£1.49	....
Know Your Traffic Signs	0 11 551612 3	£2.50	....
The Official Driving Test	0 11 552190 9	£6.99	....
The Official Driving Manual	0 11 552191 7	£12.99	....
The Official Motorcycling Manual	0 11 552193 3	£9.99	....
The Official Compulsory Basic Training	0 11 552192 5	£6.99	....
Handling charge per order:		£3.00	
	Total enclosed:	£................	

PLEASE COMPLETE IN BLOCK CAPITALS

Name ....

Address ....

....

....

.... Postcode .... | ASX |

☐ I enclose a cheque for £.................... payable to: *'The Stationery Office'*

☐ Please charge to my account with The Stationery Office, No:

....

☐ Please debit my Mastercard/Visa/Amex/Diners/Connect Card Account No.

Signature.. Expiry date ....

☐ Please send me information on TSO products. My email address is

....@..

Alternatively, contact us NOW to register at www.**clicktso**.com

☐ Please tick this box if you do not wish to receive
further information by conventional mail on
products and services from The Stationery Office.

Prices are correct at time of going to press but may be
subject to change without notice.
TSO account holders should note that credit card
transactions will not be shown on their statements.
A full listing of terms and conditions of sale can be
obtained on request from The Stationery Office
PO Box 29, Norwich NR3 1GN.

Published by The Stationery Office and available from:

The Stationery Office
(mail, telephone and fax orders only)
PO Box 29, Norwich NR3 1GN
Telephone orders/General enquiries 0870 600 5522
Fax orders 0870 600 5533

www.thestationeryoffice.com

The Stationery Office Bookshops
123 Kingsway, London WC2B 6PQ
020 7242 6393 Fax 020 7242 6394
68–69 Bull Street, Birmingham B4 6AD
0121 236 9696 Fax 0121 236 9699
33 Wine Street, Bristol BS1 2BQ
0117 926 4306 Fax 0117 929 4515
9–21 Princess Street, Manchester M60 8AS
0161 834 7201 Fax 0161 833 0634
16 Arthur Street, Belfast BT1 4GD
028 9023 8451 Fax 028 9023 5401
The Stationery Office Oriel Bookshop
18–19 High Street, Cardiff CF1 2BZ
029 2039 5548 Fax 029 2038 4347
71 Lothian Road, Edinburgh EH3 9AZ
0870 606 5566 Fax 0870 606 5588

The Stationery Office's Accredited Agents
(see Yellow Pages)

and through good booksellers

Printed in The United Kingdom for The Stationery Office TJ003154   12/00   C250   63789